PHONE TACTICS FOR INSTANT INFLUENCE

Phone Tactics for
INSTANT
INFLUENCE

John Truitt

DEMBNER BOOKS
NEW YORK

Dembner Books
Published by Red Dembner Enterprises Corp., 80 Eighth Avenue,
New York, N.Y. 10011
Distributed by W. W. Norton & Company, Inc., 500 Fifth Avenue,
New York, N.Y. 10110

Library of Congress Cataloging-in-Publication Data

Truitt. John.
Phone tactics for instant influence / John F. Truitt.
p.   cm.
ISBN 0-942637-23-2
1. Telephone etiquette.   2. Telephone in business.   I. Title.
BJ2195.T78   1990
650.1'3—dc20   89-27747
                  CIP

ACKNOWLEDGMENTS

N o one accomplishes anything worthwhile without the help of others. My wife Marisa and daughter Tesia deserve a lot of the credit, because this work could not have been completed without their constant faith, endless patience and unwavering support. There are so many friends, business associates, clients, seminar participants, and readers who over the past twenty-three years have helped me learn the skills, strategies, tactics, and techniques described in this book, that it would be impossible to name them all without running the risk of leaving someone out. This in no way diminishes the gratitude I feel, and I hope each and every one of you will accept my heartfelt thanks and appreciation for your contribution to whatever success this work may achieve.

J.T.

CONTENTS

FIGURES

1

SAVE TIME AND INFLUENCE PEOPLE WITH BETTER PHONE SKILLS

Right now anyone can pick up any telephone in America and establish instant contact with any of almost 200 million other phones in this country, plus hundreds of millions more around the world. A century and more of expanding technologies have literally put the world at our fingertips. The telephone is not only our instant link to the rest of our species, it is the greatest time-saving device ever invented for saving lives, gathering information, solving problems, collecting funds, finding help, cutting costs, creating opportunities, boosting sales, rallying support, finding employment, getting things done quickly, and much, much more.

While there are numerous techniques for using a telephone to earn money, there are even more ways it can help us save money. Simply using the guidelines in this book for comparative shopping by telephone will save the average family thousands of dollars in purchases and expenses every year. Major corporations, institutions, and government agencies can save millions.

1

Recent developments in fiber optics, microwaves, cellular systems, and satellite communications are expanding our horizons and shrinking our world. Today's telephone can either travel with us, or in many cases actually eliminate the need for transportation or travel entirely. Wherever we are, a telephone can be right there at our fingertips, ready to transport our ideas instantly to any point in the civilized world, and help us perform a myriad of functions faster, cheaper, and more productively.

Are you reaping the full benefits of all these vast resources? Do you know how to use the telephone effectively to increase your income or save your precious time and hard-earned money? Many of us take the telephone for granted, because we've grown up with it. Some even call it a nuisance. Few recognize all the potential benefits of instant access to others by phone. Even fewer know how to use it to influence other people and events in their favor. That's what *Phone Tactics for Instant Influence* is all about—how to influence other people by telephone to get immediate, positive results.

There's no question about it—some people really are more effective on the telephone than others. While some of us seem irritated or intimidated by the phone, others pick it up with confidence, immediately get through to decision makers, and seem to have total strangers eating out of their hands in a matter of seconds.

The ability to control telephone conversations is not an inborn talent; it is a combination of skills and strategies that anyone can learn and master with concentration and practice.

The purpose of this book is to teach you these skills and to show you a variety of ways to use them to save time and money in virtually every facet of your profession or home life as well. It would be impossible for one book to list all the ways you can use a telephone, but this first chapter will teach you the basic communications skills needed to control *any* telephone conversation. The remaining chapters will then provide a variety of real-life examples of the many ways you may wish to apply these skills for your own purposes. The rest is up to your imagination.

A few books have been written on telemarketing and using the phone to increase productivity at work, but isn't your time at home just as valuable? In families where both parents work, quality time at home with the children is often more precious to fathers and mothers than their time at work. In the future, personal computers, modems, and fax (facsimile) machines will make it possible for more and more Americans to work at home. Many will find their future success and total annual incomes depend to a great extent upon their ability to use the telephone productively.

Good telephone communications skills are universally applicable.

Home or office, you will use the same telephone communications skills to influence others. Once you've mastered these skills, any telephone conversation can be more productive.

How to Overcome Phone Phobias with an Edge

The most common question I hear in my seminars and TV and radio appearances is, "What about people who are naturally shy or have a phobia about calling strangers on the telephone?"

Few of us have any phobia or fear of talking to friends and relatives on the telephone. We rarely feel the need to take control of these kinds of intimate conversations either. unless we wish to avoid an argument or need a quick decision. A little INSTANT INFLU-ENCE in these situations can even save time and frustration with friends and relatives.

But some people do feel uncomfortable about calling strangers by telephone. "Butterflies" are only natural and should not be cause for concern unless they actually prevent us from making the calls we need to make. The more serious of these fears are so common in the sales profession they have a name: "call reluctance." I've actually seen salespeople, who talk with strangers face to face every day, break out in a sweat at the thought of "cold calling" by telephone.

You wouldn't be human if you didn't feel a few butterflies when making phone calls to strangers, but if you find yourself shuffling papers, making extra trips to the lounge, drinking too many cups of coffee, or finding dozens of other ways to stall instead of picking up the phone, you may be allowing normal fears to build themselves into real phobias. Constant procrastination is the most common symptom, but other people try to hide their fears by loudly expressing their impatience with telephones or their preference for dealing with people face to face. This attitude seriously limits their access to the rest of the world.

Face to face meetings are often essential, but why would any sensible person prefer to make a hassle-filled trip across town when he can accomplish everything he needs to do in a three-minute phone call? If you recognize symptoms of call reluctance in your own attitude about dealing with people over the phone . . .

Don't rationalize your fears—find the cause and correct it.

We have found in our seminars that the majority of people's phone phobias come from a lack of confidence in their ability to handle the unknown (strangers). They're not afraid of strangers per se, but they do lack confidence in *their ability* to deal effectively with them on the telephone. Most are afraid they won't know what to say, won't say it well, or will get tripped up by unexpected questions they can't answer. In other words, they have no confidence in their *phone skills.*

This lack of confidence is not a permanent handicap. It is a temporary negative mental attitude that is easily corrected by preparation—learning and then practicing good telephone communication skills. Virtually everyone in this country uses the telephone, but only a handful have ever actually studied or received any formal training in telephone communication skills or techniques of influencing other people by phone.

Earlier, I said the skills and strategies in this book will fully prepare you for virtually any conversation you will ever have on the telephone. This kind of preparation gives you confidence in your skills and a definite edge over anyone you talk with on the other end of the line. If you know *whom to call, when to call, what to say,* and *how to say it,* you will establish immediate control of your outgoing calls. Skillful use of the Teletactics (telephone tactics) described in this book will help you take charge of incoming calls with the same degree of success. You will learn the right way to handle difficult questions and have most of the answers prepared in advance. All this adds up to a very powerful advantage for controlling conversations and influencing people quickly.

Just being aware of these skills and strategies gives you an edge over other people you talk with on the telephone. Practicing them before making your calls will strengthen your confidence even more. Once you begin to use these techniques and see how easily they really work for you, your phone phobias will disappear completely—or at least be reduced to harmless butterflies that are quickly dispelled by placing your first call.

The more you know the better you will do.

Learning good telephone communications skills is a lot like learning new words. Once you know what they are, you will begin to notice them everywhere. Keep an eye out for other books and articles that emphasize good phone skills and try to emulate those who use them effectively. The more skills you learn, the greater your edge and the fewer problems you will have with call reluctance or phone phobias.

Fortify Your Confidence by Planning Ahead

You can give your confidence a real boost by planning your calls in advance. Before picking up the phone, take a minute to jot down on paper what you want to say and the questions you intend to ask. Take an extra minute to consider any questions you may be asked or information you may need to have available when you make the call. If you are preparing for a very important call or expect the conversation to be difficult or complicated, the Priority Call Planner shown below in Figure 1 should help you get ready.

Space is provided at the top of the Priority Call Planner to write in the name of the person you wish to contact, his phone number, company or organization ("of"), and his title, as well as the best time to call ("When"). Then use the left side of the form to write down the purpose of your call and your Power Opener. A Power Opener is an opening statement coupled with an initial question to help you take charge of the conversation from the start. We'll

FIGURE 1: **PRIORITY CALL PLANNER**

NAME _____ PHONE _____ EXT _____

OF _____ TITLE _____ WHEN? _____

PURPOSE OF CALL:

DATE _____ BY _____

RESULTS:

POWER OPENER:

QUESTIONS TO ASK:

NOTES & REFERRALS:

QUESTIONS TO PREPARE FOR:

INFO & REFERENCES NEEDED:

FOLLOW-UP:

discuss Power Openers in more detail in the following pages. Next list the questions you wish to ask during the conversation and try to think of any questions you may be asked at the same time. Account numbers, serial numbers, model numbers, etc., should be written down under "Info & references needed" along with a list of materials, documents, or data you will need to have at hand during the conversation.

Use the right side of the Priority Call Planner to record the date the call is completed and by whom. You may record the answers to your questions and other responses under "Results." Space is also provided for additional notes or the names and phone numbers of any references or referrals given under "Notes & referrals." Use the "Follow-up" section to record reminders for future action, follow-up calls, information to be mailed, dates for upcoming meetings and appointments, etc.

The Priority Call Planner can be used as a strategy sheet and contact record for all kinds of important business calls. It is particularly useful for planning and keeping track of sales calls, solicitations, field inquiries, progress reports, market research, credit checks, collections, follow-ups, public and customer relations, competitive bids, employee evaluations, recruiting, site and vendor selection, negotiations, conference calls, consulting assignments, and a variety of special projects as well.

Families will find the Priority Call Planner can help them prepare for important calls to builders, contractors, repairmen, lawyers, mortgage companies, landlords, schools, accountants, or the IRS (Internal Revenue Service). It can also be used for various kinds of political, church and charity work, comparative shopping, vacation planning, job hunting, school projects, or finding the best doctor, dentist, baby sitter, maid service, investment opportunities, and even tracking down rare collectibles, too.

Although it could be used for virtually any kind of telephone call imaginable, the Priority Call Planner is primarily designed for important phone calls, particularly those that could be more lengthy or complicated. You can plan simpler calls by listing the key points on a memo pad, or running through them mentally before picking up the phone. Whether you use a memo pad or a simple mental exercise, your calls will be much more effective if you make a habit of knowing these Seven Keys to Planning a Successful Phone Call *before* picking up the phone:

1. **Name and number of the person to call**
2. **Best time to call**
3. **Why you are calling**
4. **What you will say**
5. **The questions you will ask**
6. **What questions you may be asked**
7. **Facts & info to have by the phone**

This kind of advance planning will improve your confidence in your ability to handle any kind of out-going phone call successfully. It will also save a lot of time because you won't have a worry about remembering what to say next, or frantically searching for key information while you continue the conversation. Better, it will save you from having to call back a second time when you finally get your act together and have all the facts.

Avoid stress by planning ahead.

Most of the stress of call reluctance can be avoided by taking the time to plan the call in advance, as shown above. In addition, make sure you are in a comfortable spot, where you can put through your calls without the distractions of background noises and constant interruptions. Pencil and paper should be kept close to every phone, in the home or office. If you are right-handed, place the base of your phone on your left and hold the receiver in your left hand so you are free to make notes without dragging the cord across your writing materials. Lefties should keep the phone on the right and hold the receiver in the right hand for the same reason.

If you're setting appointments or arranging a meeting, you will probably need a calendar or appointment book as well. Telephone directories, call lists, or your Rolodex should be within easy reach of the phone, too.

Planning and preparation are the keys to developing the self-confidence you will need to influence other people by phone. We'll discuss specific preparations for different situations in the following chapters, but now is the time to begin forming the habit of planning your calls in advance. The more stress you eliminate in advance, the more successful your performance on the phone will be.

The Magic of Power Openers

Take the time to write out an effective Power Opener for any important phone call you have to make. Then practice saying it out loud a few times before you pick up the telephone. The Priority Call Planner shown earlier in Figure 1 should help you prepare an effective Power Opener. Remember these two points: Include the purpose of your call in your opening statement and conclude it with a question, and avoid boring the person you are calling with meaningless small talk.

Some books advise using small talk to relax strangers and get them accustomed to your voice before discussing important issues. This is fine if you are in a face to face meeting, where you have plenty of time and can use body language and your physical appearance to enhance the impression you make. Telephone conversations are different. You don't have the luxury of time and visual impressions. The best rule to follow when planning your Power Opener for a priority phone call is . . .

Get to the point immediately.

People are not likely to be sitting around waiting for your call. If they are busy doing something when the phone rings, you have five to ten seconds to get their attention, after which their thoughts will revert back to whatever they were involved in before. Forget meaningless small talk. It will cause you to lose the other person's attention before you get around to the purpose of the call.

If you lose their attention you lose control.

A carefully planned Power Opener will help establish instant control of the conversation. Some readers may wonder why this control is so important.

The ability to control a telephone conversation not only improves your confidence, it is the best way to ensure that you will get the results you want from the call.

Develop confidence in your ability to influence other people on the phone by learning to control each conversation to be certain of discussing all of the points that are important to you. The way you arrange the topics of discussion can play a major role in leading the other person to agree with your ideas and be cooperative. Controlling the conversation is also the best way to protect yourself from distractions which may either dilute the impact of your call or even cause you to forget your priorities or the major points you wish to make.

Earlier we learned that a Power Opener should consist of an opening statement coupled with a question. If you are the caller, you want to say two things in the first half of your Power Opener:

Who you are and why you called.

If you introduce yourself and state the purpose of your call in the first half of your Power Opener, the other party won't have to ask you those questions. While this may seem like a minor point it is critically important because . . .

Conversations are controlled by asking questions.

The person asking questions is always in control of the conversation, because the other party has to pause for a split second to answer. While the other party is answering the first question, the one who is controlling the conversation is already formulating his or her next question. Can you see how easy it is to direct a conversation anywhere you want it to go with a pattern of questions?

You want to be the person asking the questions rather than the one answering them. If the first half of your Power Opener states who you are and why you called, you can immediately go ahead with an initial question of your own and thus establish instant control of the conversation from the very beginning. Those who use the Priority Call Planner will have several questions prepared in advance, so they can continue the pattern until the call is successfully completed.

Occasionally you may wish to use a "choice of two" as your opening question in your Power Opener. A choice of two is preferable when you want the person you are calling to answer your opening question in a certain way. We call it a forced-response question because it is used to induce the other party to give the response we want. Salespeople often use a choice of two for arranging appointments with prospects by telephone. Below is an example of a typical Power Opener that includes a choice of two:

Jim, this is Mary Adams with XYZ Systems. I'd like to drop by your office and share some ideas with you for saving money on inventory control. Would tomorrow afternoon be convenient, or is Friday morning better for you?

Sound familiar? Notice she doesn't ask *if* the prospect wants to see her (he might say no), but *which of the two times offered is most convenient?* See what I mean about attempting to force a desired response?

The following chapters are full of examples of effective Power Openers and forced-response questions for all kinds of situations. Just remember . . .

No Power Opener is complete without a question.

In fact, if you forget to use a question with your opening statement, you won't have any power at all. You will not only miss your best opportunity for establishing instant control of the conversation, but may in fact lose control to the other party instead. Form the habit of using a Power Opener that states who you are, why you called, and ends in either a simple, direct question or choice of two. Practice saying it out loud with the kind of Telestyle we'll discuss in the next few paragraphs until you are comfortable "wrapping your mouth around the words" and are satisfied with how they sound. People will be impressed with your professionalism, and you will have a much easier time of controlling the conversation the way you want to. That's the magic of a good Power Opener.

Elements of Telestyle

Your style of speaking on the telephone is what I refer to as your Telestyle. You want to speak clearly and distinctly so that others can understand you. The mouthpiece of your telephone should be close enough to your mouth to pick up the tone of your voice, but not too close or your voice will have a hissing sound that will distort your words. If you hold it too far away, you will sound too distant. Two inches is the proper distance. That is about the width of three fingers held close together between your mouth and the mouthpiece of the phone.

The mood of any telephone conversation, even between strangers, is established in the beginning. If the person who initiates the call uses a friendly, upbeat, and cheerful Telestyle, the other party will react in the same manner. If on the other hand the caller is angry, mean, or impatient, whoever answers the phone will act that way too. Because this emotional reaction is instantaneous, anyone interested in controlling a telephone conversation should be careful to convey the mood he wants from the start. One of the secrets of influencing other people on the phone is to create a friendly relationship and spirit of cooperation.

The best way to begin a friendly conversation is to <u>assume familiarity</u> and <u>smile</u>.

Obviously the other party can't see your smile, but he can hear it in your voice. Radio announcers have practiced this technique for years in order to make their voices sound friendlier and more pleasant on the air. "Assuming familiarity" means acting as if you and the other party already are friends. Using his or her first name is particularly helpful when you want to eliminate formalities and "personalize" a conversation between two professionals. If you don't know the name of the person you are calling beforehand, you can always ask whoever answers the phone when you call. For example . . .

Receptionist: "XYZ Company; may I help you?"
Caller: "Hi, this is John Truitt. Who am I speaking with, please?"

Receptionist: "This is Jane Smith."

Caller: "Jane, I need to speak with someone in customer service. Can you tell me who's in charge of that department, please?"

Receptionist: "That would be Mr. Johnson. May I transfer your call?"

Caller: "Before you do, can you tell me his first name or what his friends call him?"

Receptionist: "His first name is James, but everybody in the office calls him Jim. May I connect you now?"

We'll discuss more ways of obtaining first names later, but as you can see this is not too difficult at all.

While Mr. or Ms. may be more appropriate with customers and with people much older than you, assuming the familiarity of a first name and smiling as you speak in a friendly manner will help you avoid lengthy introductions and some of the formalities, skepticism, or suspicions that are only natural between strangers. Your friendly attitude diffuses tensions instantly by producing a congenial response from the other party, and helps ensure that you will both talk *to* each other rather than *at* each other. This is the kind of communication that produces INSTANT INFLUENCE from the very beginning.

A friendly, cheerful Telestyle is just as important when answering the phone as it is when you are the caller. Even the most irate callers can be soothed into a better spirit of cooperation with a smile. In fact we always advise secretaries and receptionists who attend our seminars to place a small mirror on their desk by the phone to help them remember to smile when answering the phone. A mirror is just as helpful for those placing outgoing calls, too. A friendly voice on the telephone is the least expensive, yet most effective, method I know of for presenting a positive corporate image to anyone on the other end of the phone line. All you have to do is *smile*.

Your Secret Weapon

Many people never realize the importance of emotions in a phone call, yet most human beings react much faster to emotional impulses than they do to logic or reason. We all prefer to think we do things because they are reasonable, but in reality most of us do what we do because of how we "feel" about it at the time.

The way to influence people is to make them <u>want</u> to help you.

It is much easier to *motivate* people to want to do something than it is to intimidate or force them, particularly from a distance over the telephone. People are typically skeptical of others' methods or quality of reasoning—particularly those of persons they don't know. If you doubt this, just remember the last time you thought you were stating an irrefutable fact, which ended up causing an argument.

Most telephone conversations start quickly and are so brief that we don't have time for proofs and theorems, much less lengthy discussions or arguments. Rather than lament the brevity of such calls, we can instead capitalize upon it by creating the mood of the entire conversation in an instant. The easiest way to motivate people is to get them excited about your project. The best way to get other people excited is to be excited yourself. In other words . . .

Speak with enthusiasm.

Nothing has a greater impact than enthusiasm when it comes to influencing people quickly. Enthusiasm is unbelievably contagious on the telephone. No matter what you're talking about, if you are excited about your topic, the person you are speaking to will also become excited—even if he or she is a total stranger or might normally disagree with you. I know this may not sound logical, but it is a basic characteristic of human nature.

If you say your Power Opener with a friendly, cheerful, enthusiastic Telestyle, others will instantly react in the same manner without ever thinking about why.

Enthusiasm is your secret weapon when it comes to influencing other people or being persuasive. Some readers may question their ability to sound excited or turn on their own enthusiasm at will. This will not be difficult at all if you remember to . . .

<u>Slightly</u> raise the volume and speed of your voice.

If you find yourself in a conversation going nowhere, turn on the enthusiasm and watch what happens. The other party will begin to react to your excitement instantly, by becoming as excited as you are. Notice I said *slightly* raise the volume and speed of your voice. Don't shout or speak so fast that the other person can't understand what you are saying. A slight increase in volume and speed is all that is necessary to produce the enthusiasm you need. You will immediately notice the difference in the other person's reaction. Actually he or she will not be reacting to *what* you are saying, but *how* you are speaking. A friendly, enthusiastic Telestyle will overcome a multitude of mistakes and help you win friends and influence people quickly over the telephone. This kind of INSTANT INFLUENCE almost always produces positive results.

Preparations for Teletactics

Although an effective Power Opener and a friendly, enthusiastic Telestyle will help you take charge of virtually any telephone conversation, you must also be prepared for questions or objections from the other party. Otherwise you may find yourself losing control in the middle of the discussion. Those answering the phone are even more vulnerable to questions from callers. How do you defend yourself and seize control of the conversation at the same time?

You could of course follow what we call the Politician's Ploy and answer questions with questions, but you will run the risk of sounding evasive. Politicians do. If instead you follow what we have called Truitt's Law, you can answer difficult questions without sounding evasive, and still use questions of your own to recapture control of the conversation.

Truitt's Law:

Answer the other person's question, but finish your answer with a question of your own to regain control of the conversation.

Earlier we stated that the person who is asking the questions is always in control of the conversation. There are a variety of Teletactics like Truitt's Law and the Politician's Ploy that help you maintain control throughout the entire conversation. Once again . . .

Preparation is the key to success.

If you use the Priority Call Planner, space is provided for writing down the most likely questions or objections you could receive from the person you are calling. This allows you to look at the question objectively and develop a proper response beforehand. You can also do this for many of the calls you are likely to receive.

If, for example, you have advertised an employment opening in the classifieds, or a "For Sale by Owner" listing, you will be expecting certain questions from respondents. Have your answers ready. The same would apply to companies who include toll-free numbers in their sales literature, TV and radio commercials, direct mail, or other forms of direct response advertising. If you are in business you will often receive calls from prospective customers inquiring about your products or services, too. Be prepared to supply the information. Whether you are placing or answering phone calls, there are numerous occasions when certain questions are to be expected, and nothing makes a better impression than having the facts on hand.

Prepare for expected questions in advance.

It is much easier to develop good answers to questions when you have time to prepare for them than during the haste of a two- or three-minute phone call. The following chapters will give you a lot of answers to the most common questions you are likely to receive under various circumstances. Those answers should provide you with more ideas of ways to handle other situations.

If you expect certain questions, plan your responses in advance and practice saying them over a few times until you are satisfied with your delivery. In fact, why not plan beforehand for the worst or most difficult questions you could possibly be asked? Then you will be ready for anything. Don't forget to have a couple of questions of your own prepared in advance so you can regain control of the conversation. Can you see how this improves your edge?

The next chapters will discuss ways of answering calls for both businesses and residences as well. If you're in business, train your staff to handle normal inquiries and unexpected questions properly, and let them practice among themselves until you are not only satisfied with their answers, but the overall corporate image they are projecting as well. Use the same methods to teach children and other family members how to answer your home phone properly and handle difficult questions effectively. This is not only important for business calls at home; it can significantly improve your home security as well.

When a phone call is unexpected and the caller asks a difficult question, good phone skills and Teletactics like Truitt's Law and the Politician's Ploy are your best defenses. Obviously you can't have specific answers prepared in advance, but the more you develop the habit of phrasing your answers with questions of your own to maintain control of conversations, the easier it will be to handle the unexpected.

When to Use the Reverse

The inability to handle difficult questions is the most common reason most people lose control of a telephone conversation, but arguments are by far the most destructive. One party makes a statement that the other disagrees with, and the debate that follows is a total waste of time for everyone. Rarely does anyone ever win an argument over the telephone without costing himself time and/or money and a good relationship with the other party.

An argument can be particularly costly to a sales or service person at odds with a customer. Sure, he may win the argument, but he will probably lose the customer. Although it takes a little willpower and self-control, the Reverse is one of the best Teletactics I know of for avoiding arguments and actually winning agreement with a party holding a differing point of view. If you find yourself in disagreement with the other party, don't immediately protest or jump to the defense of your idea. Instead, use the Reverse.

Smile and do the unexpected—agree.

No, you don't have to lie or agree with something you know is wrong, but you can remain friendly as you make your own point in an agreeable manner. For example:

Caller: "Oh, I can certainly understand how you might feel that way, but why not consider this too . . . ?"

or

"Sure, and if we follow this plan . . ."

or

"I can understand that, and we could improve upon it if . . ."

If you find yourself in disagreement with someone, but you have a strong reason for persuading him to go along with what you want, the Reverse is a powerful maneuver. Any little statement like "I understand," "sure," or "I see what you mean" sounds agreeable and will immediately diffuse tensions, while setting a more receptive stage for the points you wish to make. It is almost impossible for even the most stubborn debaters to continue an argument with someone who keeps agreeing with them. Combine the Reverse with a cheerful, enthusiastic Telestyle, and you will be amazed at how productive the most difficult discussions can be.

The Reverse can be particularly useful for soothing irate customers and handling complaints. Most of these discussions would be more productive if whoever answers the call would handle the complaint more courteously with a simple statement of agreement like, "I'm sorry you've had so much trouble with one of our products. Let me connect you with someone who can help you . . ."

We'll demonstrate a number of ways to use the Reverse in the following chapters, but for now start getting in the habit of avoiding arguments on the telephone. Just remember that disagreements and heated discussions are costly and lead nowhere. If you find yourself in danger of becoming embroiled in an argument, use the Reverse to keep the conversation friendly, and take the time to listen to the other party's point of view.

The Importance of Listening

Sure it takes willpower to be silent when someone is saying something you are vehemently opposed to, but if you listen without interrupting, you will learn something you don't already know—either about the topic of discussion or about the other party. This knowledge may cause you to change your own position, or it may reveal a way to motivate the other person to go along with you anyway. "Knowledge is power" as the old saying goes—and "the more you listen the more you learn" seems appropriate here, too.

If you are a good listener, you will allow the other party to "talk out" his opposition. Many people simply want a hearing. Once their objections are known, they are often willing to have them disproved or overcome with a better idea. People like to express their opinions and feel those opinions are taken seriously. They also enjoy talking about themselves and their problems. Be a good listener, and others will think you are the best conversationalist they've ever met. The more they respect you, the more they will appreciate your ideas and the easier time you will have of using INSTANT INFLUENCE to get the results you want from the call.

Learn to Control Your Attitude

PMA (positive mental attitude) is critical for anyone hoping to influence others—particularly by phone. I define PMA this way:

A "positive mental attitude" is the belief that, with the proper training and proper materials, one can accomplish anything he or she sets out to do.

The purpose of this book is to help you develop the PMA you need to handle calls successfully. The more skills you learn and master with practice, the easier it will be to maintain a positive attitude when you run into obstacles.

A positive attitude allows you to think clearly during telephone discussions and use the skills you have learned here to maintain control. If you become flustered, confused, or irritated, you'll only end up reacting to what others do instead of influencing them yourself. Controlling your attitude always makes it easier to remember useful Teletactics like listening, the Reverse, and Truitt's Law when you need them.

Keep a friendly, positive attitude when using the phone and never allow the negative reactions or responses of others to change it.

If you learn to control your attitude and keep it friendly, you will always come out a winner in the end, regardless of what others do.

Focus Your Conversation for INSTANT INFLUENCE

One of the best reasons for writing down the purpose of your call on the Priority Call Planner is to help you avoid getting sidetracked during the discussion. Having it written in front of you during the call helps you keep the conversation focused upon your own priorities. No matter where the discussion leads, you can always get back to the points that are important to you if you have written them down in advance.

If on the other hand you allow yourself to be distracted, you will find it difficult, if not impossible, to exercise any influence at all. Consider consumers who feel they have been ripped-off by a shady business. High-pressure salesmen, con artists, and other unethical business people are masters of distraction when it comes to handling customer complaints. They will employ a variety of tactics to avoid canceling orders, correcting problems, or paying out refunds. Why not beat them at their own game and frustrate *them* with phone skills?

Anyone you talk with on the telephone will appreciate your professionalism if you ignore distractions and stay on track.

Small talk is a distraction.

Naturally you want to enjoy a friendly relationship with others on the phone, but if you allow the discussion to ramble, you may never get to the points you need to discuss. Maintain a friendly attitude during the entire conversation, but save the chitchat for after you've gotten the results you want. This way your calls can be friendly and more productive at the same time.

Keeping the conversation focused upon the important points will not only improve your overall results, it will also save everyone's time.

Respect for the value of time is a sure sign of professionalism. Avoid rambling discussions whenever you can, and people will be impressed with your organizational skills and efficiency, as well as your demonstrated respect for them. The more professional you sound on the telephone, the easier it will be to influence others.

Teach Yourself the Basics

Throughout this chapter we have discussed forming good habits in the beginning. Planning your calls, preparing questions and answers in advance, smiling, using questions for control, and maintaining a positive mental attitude are all habits you can form with practice. Begin to form these habits now. Once they become natural to you, all of your phone calls will be more productive. The Call Review Checklist shown in Figure 2 should help remind you of the basic phone skills we've discussed and the habits that lead to success.

The Call Review Checklist can help you evaluate your perfor-

FIGURE 2: **CALL REVIEW CHECKLIST**

Answer the following questions as honestly and objectively as you can to
review your call and see where you may need to improve your skills:

Did you . . .

	Yes	No	
1.			Outline the purpose of your call in advance?
2.			Use a Power Opener (with an opening question)?
3.			Practice your Power Opener before calling?
4.			List the questions you meant to ask in advance?
5.			Prepare for questions from others?
6.			Get to the point immediately?
7.			Smile and assume familiarity?
8.			Speak with enthusiasm?
9.			Control the conversation with questions?
10.			Offer a choice of two when appropriate?
11.			Use Truitt's Law to handle difficult questions?
12.			Use the Reverse to avoid arguments?
13.			Remember to listen to the other party?
14.			Control your attitude?
15.			Focus your conversation on your priorities?
16.			Practice good phone skills persistently?
17.			Cover all the points you wanted to?
18.			Achieve all of your objectives with the call?

If you answered yes to all eighteen questions you had a very productive
phone call. Any no's should indicate the skills you need to review and
practice.

Remember . . .

The more you practice the more your skills will improve.

mance after any phone call you wish to analyze. The more you use it, the more questions on the list you will be able to answer with a yes, and the faster your confidence will grow. Since the no's stand out, weaknesses will be instantly highlighted for you to work on.

Use the Priority Call Planner (Figure 1) to prepare for the call in advance, then evaluate your phone skills afterward with the Call Review Checklist (Figure 2). Keep the two forms in front of you when you are placing important phone calls, and you quickly can teach yourself to be more effective on the telephone.

Chances are you have already learned enough by now to improve your telephone effectiveness significantly. Knowing the skills that count gives you an edge over most of the people you will talk with on the phone in the future. The following chapters are filled with examples of how to apply these skills in everyday situations. Sample dialogues include Power Openers, Reverses, and other Teletactics, along with a variety of questions and answers that should help to increase your advantage even more.

Practice repeating your "lines" out loud like an actor rehearsing for a performance. Your own performance on the phone will improve significantly. Role-playing with a friend, co-worker, spouse, or even by yourself is an excellent way to learn the basics of INSTANT INFLUENCE quickly.

A tape recorder is a valuable training aid. You may wish to invest in a telephone "pick-up" device to tape your actual phone calls, for a more accurate review of your techniques. These are available in most electronics stores and are particularly handy for recording complicated discussions.

Persistence Pays Big Dividends

Some readers may experience a few awkward moments at first in implementing the skills and strategies outlined in this book. Learning good telephone communications skills, like anything else, takes time and practice. If you find your first attempts at INSTANT INFLUENCE are shaky, don't give up. It will get easier as you go along.

Not only will you soon feel comfortable on the telephone, but you will even look forward to finding additional ways to use your skills more productively. I've taught many of the techniques described in this book to all kinds of people for over twenty years. Most had average speaking skills, but some even stuttered, others appeared shy or introverted at first, and a few barely spoke English. Yet those who invested effort in learning always succeeded.

If you don't quit trying, you will not fail.

The following chapters will show you how to save time doing virtually anything you want with any home or business telephone. Refer back to this chapter as often as you like to review your basic skills. Practice these techniques until they become second nature. You will soon be amazed at how easily and quickly you can influence people and events with the telephone. As always . . .

Planning, practice and persistent effort with a positive mental attitude will ultimately win success in any endeavor.

2

THE
TOP TEN PRIORITIES
FOR ANSWERING
BUSINESS PHONES

Who can even begin to count the number of business deals proposed and closed over the world's telephones every day? Your business phone is your direct line of instant communications— with the rest of your own organization and with the rest of the world. Often as not, most of your first conversations with customers will occur over the telephone, if only to set an appointment, answer an inquiry, give someone your mailing address or directions for finding your place of business.

Superior phone skills will project your best front office appearance. Considering how much time, effort, and money we invest in attracting new customers and building a positive corporate image, it is easy to see the importance of answering our business phones with warmth and encouragement.

Technology can't offer the personal touch.

Here's irony for you. Today, some companies are spending millions of dollars on advertising, promotions, and public relations to attract new customers. Then they turn around and try to save a few thousand by using automated systems instead of people to answer their phones when those new customers call. Computers and answering machines are confusing to anyone unfamiliar with them, and particularly frustrating to those in a hurry to speak with a decision maker. Most callers confronted with a recorded message will just hang up and call another firm. Others may reason that if a company is so impersonal before the sale, how much more aloof will it be after it has taken the customer's money?

Companies which let machines answer their incoming calls miss forever an invaluable opportunity. You get only one chance to create a dynamic first impression. Automated answering machines, electronic mail systems, and computer message centers are great time and money savers when used properly, but if possible . . .

Don't let a machine answer your publicly listed business phone during normal office hours.

Tremendous strides toward more accurate message taking and faster communications have been made by forward-thinking companies who use automated phone systems. But their telephones are first answered by professional operators with pleasant cheerful phone voices. When necessary, they introduce the caller to their automated systems *before* routing the call to a computerized message center.

Operator: "I'm sorry, Mr. Johnson doesn't answer his direct line, but you can leave your name and number with our computerized message center, and he'll get back to you as soon as possible. It's easy to use. May I connect you now?"

or

"Yes, Mr. Truitt, I'll be happy to connect you with Mr. Johnson's office. But if he's not available, his automated message system will help you get word to him faster than I can. Will you hold for a moment please?"

A little extra effort when answering the phone can help any company or business take full advantage of modern technology, while projecting an attractive and personable image. After all, one of the first rules of any successful enterprise is . . .

Be *easy* to do business with.

The easier your firm is to deal with, the more repeat business you will develop. If your competitors are using computers and machines to handle their phone traffic mechanically, you can actually take customers away from them by using real people to answer your phone. All they need is a friendly, cheerful, enthusiastic Telestyle.

Begin teaching employees how to influence incoming calls by explaining what we call the Top Ten Priorities for Answering Business Phones. We all learn much faster when we understand which tactics are important to remember and the reasons for their importance. Of course the first thing your employees will have to remember is . . .

Priority No. 1: Answer Your Business Calls on the First or Second Ring.

You want to reinforce your image of a business that is instantly available and always ready to provide the service your clients deserve—fast, efficient, personal. If whoever handles your business phones is too busy to answer quickly, consider redistributing his or her workload, or hire extra help. Let your competitors complain about the difficulties of handling their phone traffic promptly while you take steps to solve the problem and avoid appearing cheap, unreliable or slovenly. Remember . . .

If you make potential customers wait too long, they'll just call your competitor.

Today's rapidly expanding service industry indicates that in the future . . .

Success in business will be spelled s-e-r-v-i-c-e.

Today the service industry is the fastest growing segment of the world economy. Even suppliers of food products, raw materials, and manufactured goods emphasize their ability to service their customers' needs efficiently. The age of computers, fax machines, and cellular phones is creating a tidal wave of new and faster services for the future.

Superior service begins with swift attention to the needs of your clients.

A caller's first impression of your firm starts when you answer the phone. Simply answering on the first or second ring shows that you are alert and gives an immediate impression of fast, efficient service and quality products.

The next few paragraphs will help you add a personal touch to this impression, because . . .

As automation takes over more and more of our daily lives, those businesses that are able to personalize their services will achieve the greatest success.

The more impersonal business becomes, the more people will appreciate the unique enterprise that successfully combines technology with a personal touch.

Priority No. 2: Create a Positive First Impression with a Smiling Telestyle.

One of the best examples of a corporation using effective Telestyle is Delta Airlines. Over the years, Delta has earned a reputation for top quality service and happy employees who take a lot of pride in their work. (A few years ago, while most airlines were experiencing tremendous labor problems, Delta's employees purchased a jumbo jet and then gave it to their employer.) That is exactly the way they sound when they answer their phones, too—

Bright, cheerful, friendly, courteous, and sincerely interested in offering the highest quality service.

I can think of no better first impression any business could make in just five seconds. This is INSTANT INFLUENCE for profit.

What kind of impression do those answering your business phones project? Do they sound friendly? Or intimidating? Cheerful? Or bored? Helpful? Or tired? Confident? Or angry? Frustrated? Combative? Ignorant? Callous?

We get only one chance to make a good first impression, yet first impressions are often the most lasting and influential.

Many psychologists agree that first impressions influence our opinions about a person or enterprise immediately, and often carry the most weight during the decision-making processes. Are first impressions important if one is "only an employee?"

The caller's first impression of <u>you</u> is always important.

Whenever your business phone rings, you personally have an opportunity to shine. In just five to ten seconds, you can demonstrate that you are bright, cheerful, and enthusiastic about your work, proud of your employer and sincerely interested in helping the caller deal with your firm in a friendly and efficient manner.

Earn your pay.

If answering your employer's phone is your job—or part of your job—then you certainly owe it to him to do the best you can at it. Take pride in the quality of your work. Answer the phone with enthusiasm, confidence, and a big smile.

Anyone who answers a business phone is the firm's instant public relations representative.

Answering the phone in a friendly, cheerful, helpful manner may not only earn you a raise, but may ultimately affect the paychecks of all your company's employees.

The better your firm's public image, the more successful it will be. The more successful a firm becomes, the more it can afford to pay its employees.

Your company's image rubs off on you. Just as the caller's first impression of you will influence his or her impression of your company, so too the caller's first impression of your company will affect his or her first impression of you. Most of us feel that sharp companies employ sharp people (and vice versa, too). Your employment by a successful enterprise will automatically lead people to believe that you are succeeding in your career, too.

Good Telestyle makes it easier to establish control.

In the preceding chapter we discussed how a smile makes your voice sound friendlier. So, keep a mirror on your desk to make sure you remember to smile when the phone rings so that you will answer like a friend. If you smile when answering your business phone and speak in a cheerful, enthusiastic manner . . .

You will momentarily brighten the day of any caller.

The way you answer your business phone will set the mood for the entire conversation. Regardless of who is calling, if you really want to influence other people quickly on the telephone . . .

Begin each conversation by making the caller feel good about talking with you.

If you are friendly, it is natural for the caller to respond in the same manner. You will immediately begin to gain his trust and respect, and this really does make it easier to control the conversation. It also helps you obtain whatever information you need to handle the call more productively. Guarded or hostile callers can be softened by a friendly approach and thus made cooperative. The rest of the conversation will be a lot more pleasant for both parties if it starts out right in the beginning.

Some people say it helps to picture callers in their minds when they answer their phones. Basically there are two kinds of callers:

those who know you and those who don't. Since we have no way of identifying the caller in advance, the logical strategy to follow is to . . .

Answer the phone as if the caller is your firm's best customer.

If it really is your best customer he will appreciate such a warm greeting and all other callers will appreciate red-carpet treatment too, and may someday become some of your firm's best customers.

Of course, many of your calls will be from other employees, branch offices, job hunters, suppliers and vendors, etc. But the same best-customer greeting will also help you establish control of conversations with them. It can impress your boss and other managers with your firm, as well as their friends and business associates. Their comments about your phone skills will not only help you gain recognition, but may help you earn a promotion or pay raise, too.

Priority No. 3: Use a Prepared Introduction When Answering Your Business Phone.

Unless you have a reason for maintaining confidentiality or you are using a residence phone for business purposes . . .

State the name of your firm in your introduction.

Answering your business phone is simply one more opportunity for getting the name of your enterprise firmly implanted in the conscious and subconscious minds of the public. It's also free.

Except for stating the name of your firm, the words you use to answer your business phone are not nearly as important as the way you use them. Be original if you wish, but don't get too cutesy—many people regard gimmicky responses as unprofessional. Write out a brief introduction that you can repeat comfortably with feeling when you answer the phone. Just be yourself, but be the friendliest, most cheerful self you can be. The following are a few examples of successful introductions used by various businesses:

"XYZ Company. This is Jim Johnson . . . May I help you?"

"Executive Search Consultants . . .?"

"State Employment Office. May I have the extension you are calling, please?"

"Dr. Clark's Office. This is Judy Johnson . . . May I help you?"

"Thank you for calling Telestar Inc. This is John Truitt . . . May I help you?"

"Joe's Garage . . . Who's calling, please?"

As you can see, originality is not necessary. Giving the company name along with both your first and last name personalizes the conversation and also implies honesty by demonstrating your willingness to identify yourself. Enthusiasm implies efficiency, professionalism and pride in your work and an eagerness to serve. "Thank you for calling" shows that you do appreciate the opportunity to serve the caller. Simply stating the name of the company (with a smile) when you pick up the phone sounds professional and friendly, too. The question "may I help you?" further conveys your willingness and also helps establish control of the conversation.

Don't try to say too much when you answer the phone. If your company name is a mouthful in itself, then that's probably all you should say in your introduction.

"Baldwin, Jackson, Anderson, and Bullwinkle . . . ?"

Occasionally the need for confidentiality may require that the name of our firm not be revealed when answering a business phone. For example, the company may be conducting a executive search or running a "blind ad" in the employment section of a newspaper. One of the following examples may help you answer a "blind number" phone:

"Yes, may I help you?"

"Executive offices. May I help you?"

"Yes?"

If you are answering an extension phone in a private office or department (after callers have already gone through your main switchboard), there is no need to repeat the name of your firm. But you can add a personal touch by introducing yourself when you pick up the phone.

> **"Customer service. This is Joan Collins. May I help you?"**

If you're an executive answering your own extension (or cellular phone), just state your name.

> **"This is John Truitt."**

If you've been told the name of the party waiting to speak with you, make it a friendlier greeting:

> **"Good morning, Mr. Phelps. This is John Truitt. What can I do for you?"**

If you're an assistant answering the phone for an executive's private office . . .

> **"Ms. Johnson's office. This is Joe Baker. May I help you?"**

For a group of executives:

> **"Executive offices. This is Mary Taylor. May I help you?"**

Plan a brief introduction that makes it easy to say what you want, and practice saying it out loud a few times until you are satisfied with your delivery. Use any of the above introductions that suits your needs and say it with a smiling, enthusiastic Telestyle, and you will create a great first impression. Finish your statement with a question like "May I help you?", "May I have the extension you are calling, please?", or "Who's calling, please?" and you will have initiated control of the conversation that follows, too.

Companies that employ several operators to handle their incoming calls can significantly improve their efficiency by making sure each operator (receptionist or secretary) has an introduction prepared in advance, with a question designed to process incoming calls faster:

> **"XYZ Company. This is Judy Johnson. May I have the extension you're calling please?"**
>
> **"Executive Search Consultants. Who's calling, please?"**
>
> **"Master Service. This is Bill Thompson. May I have your account number first, please?"**

A question with your prepared introduction is not absolutely essential, because the caller is going to say something or make a request after you answer the phone anyway. However, it can help you direct the flow of the conversation faster, thereby saving your time so you can handle more calls during the day. Remember to smile and speak with a very cheerful telestyle when using these techniques, so they won't sound brusque or overly aggressive.

Priority No. 4: Identify the Caller and Repeat the Name as Soon as It Is Given.

"Who is calling?" is probably the first question you will have to ask. Of course if you are handling a large switchboard, there is no need for you to know the caller's name—whoever answers the extension will take care of that. You need to ask only the name or extension of the party the caller wishes to talk with. If, on the other hand, you are handling incoming calls for a small department or private office, you may be required to find out the caller's name (and more) before putting it through.

> **"Mr. Johnson's office. May I say who's calling, please?"**

Whether the caller volunteers his name or you ask for it . . .

Repeat the caller's name as soon as it is given.

This not only helps you remember the name, but allows you an opportunity to show special courtesy. People appreciate courtesies and respect. If you don't understand the name, ask for it again, rather than run the risk of insulting the caller by mispronouncing his or her name . . .

> **Operator: "I'm sorry. Would you mind repeating your name, please?"**

Some callers will immediately identify themselves when you answer the phone.

> **Caller: "This is John Truitt for Jim Johnson. Is he in?"**

I teach this kind of Power Opener because it is more courteous, saves time establishing control of the conversation, and makes it easy for whoever answers the phone to handle the call properly. Just continue the conversation like this:

> **Operator: "I'll be glad to check for you, Mr. Truitt. Can you hold for a moment, please?"**
>
> If you want to take charge of the call for screening purposes, handle it this way:
>
> **"I'll be glad to see if he's in, Mr. Truitt. Will he know what your call is about?"**

We'll talk about screening calls later. For now, if you identify the caller immediately, and then repeat the name as soon as it is given, you won't have to worry about forgetting the name. Addressing callers by name also reinforces your firm's image of offering a personal touch.

Priority No. 5: Be a Model of Proper Etiquette and Courtesy.

Use the proper "Mr." or "Ms." when you repeat the caller's last name and continue to address the caller in the same manner throughout the conversation. Use "please" and "thank you" whenever appropriate, and the caller will appreciate the obvious respect and deferential treatment he or she is receiving from you. These are simple professional courtesies, which cost you nothing to extend, but can help make a big impression with callers.

Priority No. 6: Determine the Purpose of the Call as It Relates to you.

Here again if you're on the main switchboard of a major corporation, "determining the purpose of the call" may simply mean finding out the name of the person and the department or extension the caller is trying to reach. This information is usually volunteered by callers as soon as you answer the phone.

Some callers may not know which party they need to speak with. If your employer has an information desk, refer the call there.

> **Operator: "Our information operator can probably give you the name of the person who can help you. Would you mind holding for a moment while I transfer your call?"**

If, however, you are the person responsible for routing incoming calls, you will have to determine the purpose of the call yourself.

> **"I'll be glad to connect you with someone who can help you, Mr. Thompson. If you can give me an idea of the type of assistance you're looking for . . . or was there a particular question you wanted to ask?"**
>
> **"Let me see who's available, Mr. Thompson. Can you tell me what the call is about, please?"**

Once you know the purpose of the call, there are basically four ways to handle it:

1. **Transfer the call to someone else.**
2. **Take a message (if the party called is unavailable).**
3. **Help the caller yourself.**
4. **Screen the call.**

If you're going to ask the caller to hold while you transfer the call to someone else, remember . . .

Priority No. 7: Respect the Value of the Caller's Time.

One of the easiest ways to anger a caller is to waste his or her time—particularly by leaving him on hold for an extended period of time. Musak doesn't help either. In fact, whenever I'm asked to hold and music comes on, I know it's going to be a long wait, so I hang up. Even worse is a recorded sales pitch about all the company's products.

Once an appliance dealer played the local radio broadcast over the line while I was holding for the manager. Another appliance firm's radio commercial sounded so good that I hung up the phone and called the competitor instead. A friend learned from a newscast he heard while waiting on the line that the firm he was calling was being sued for misrepresentation. Needless to say, he didn't hold much longer, either!

Music, radio programming, and recorded messages are sure-fire ways of letting callers know that you are going to waste a lot of their time.

Companies would be wiser to invest in training employees (or adding more) to handle their phone calls more efficiently.

The more efficiently you service your customers' needs, the more customers you'll be asked to serve.

Before asking any caller to hold for an extended period of time . . .

Offer to take a message. Then have the call returned as soon as someone is free.

This is an easy way to avoid irritating callers and provide a better service, too. If callers choose to hold anyway . . .

Check with callers who are holding at thirty-second intervals, to let them know that they haven't been forgotten.

This kind of courtesy shows your firm's respect for the value of the caller's time, and proves that you care about the quality of service you are providing.

Use a "choice of two" if you want to influence the caller either to continue holding or to leave a message. If you'd prefer to take a message and get the caller off the line . . .

> **Operator: "I guess Mr. Truitt is away from his desk right now, Ms. Roberts. Do you have time to continue holding? Or would you rather leave a message so he can return your call as soon as he gets back?"**

> If you want a caller to continue holding, say it this way . . .

> **"I'm sorry it's taking so long, Mr. Thompson. I'll be glad to take a message for you. Or if you don't mind holding a little longer, Mr. Truitt should be with you shortly. Which would you prefer?"**

Most callers will be naturally inclined to select the second of a choice of two, because it is said last. It sounds like the one you are emphasizing, and they hear it more clearly, too. This is a great Teletactic for avoiding irritating a caller who must be put on hold. If the caller is given a choice and chooses to hold, he or she is less likely to resent the extra time it takes.

Priority No. 8: Use Friendly Questions to Establish and Maintain Control.

Once the caller identifies himself, states the purpose of his call, asks for someone else, or says anything at all, you will then want to seize immediate control of the conversation with questions of your own:

> **Operator: "I'll be happy to connect you with Mr. Truitt's office. May I tell him who's calling, please?"**
>
> **"Our customer service department will be glad to help you, Ms. King. Can you please hold for a moment while I connect you?"**
>
> **"Yes, are you calling about the ad in the paper?"**
>
> **"He's not in right now, Mr. O'Brien. Would you like me to connect you with his message center?"**
>
> **"I'll be happy to help you with that. Who's calling please?"**
>
> **"Yes, he's in, Mr. Bassham. May I prepare him for the nature of your call?"**

"Who's calling, please?", "What company are you with?", "What is the nature of your call?", "Would you hold for a moment, please?", "May I give him a message?", and "Does he know you?" are all questions you can ask to establish immediate control of incoming calls. In fact virtually any logical question can be used to establish control, but remember to pose it in a friendly, cheerful manner so you don't sound crass, overly nosy, or difficult to do business with. Don't hit the caller with a barrage of questions, either.

Use just enough questions to obtain whatever information you need to control the conversation.

Too many questions can irritate callers who may be in a hurry. Make sure the questions you are asking are necessary and remember your Telestyle:

Impression + Control = <u>Instant Influence</u>

We've already discussed how you can use Telestyle to create a positive first impression. Asking friendly questions, as you lead the caller to cooperate and furnish the information you need to handle the call, will back up that good first impression.

Priority No. 9: Be Prepared to Process Messages Accurately and Fast.

Most people can take messages with reasonable accuracy when business is slow. But are your employees prepared to take accurate messages when other phone lines are flashing, people are rushing in and out, and noisy business machines are running in the background? Whoever organizes your offices and directs your telecommunications should have a plan in place for processing messages among all departments. Many companies have message centers. Some are quite large with several professional operators, while others rely upon computers and automated systems. Many small organizations will simply designate one person's desk (usually the receptionist or office manager) as their message center. Those who handle messages in person should always . . .

Post messages promptly in the same place.

Whether your company uses an automated system or a specially designated employee to take messages, other employees should . . .

Form the habit of checking for messages regularly.

Regardless of the size of the organization you work for or the degree of its automation, you will still need to take written messages yourself from time to time.

Assign someone to make sure pencils and paper (or your firm's message pads) are always kept beside every phone in your organization.

Handy writing materials are a godsend when things are hectic.

Accurate message taking is a professional skill.

Of all the plaques and quotations in my cluttered office, the most prominently displayed is a statement of Bacon's: "I hold every man a debtor to his profession, from the which, as men of course do seek to receive countenance and profit, so ought they of duty to endeavor themselves, by way of amends, to be a help and ornament thereunto."

I believe the concept of being a "debtor to one's profession" is the basic foundation of true professionalism—caring enough about what we do to master all the basics and perform them as well as we can. Accurate message taking is a necessary professional skill in any occupation. When practiced efficiently, it definitely will make you "a help and ornament thereunto" any business or professional organization employing you.

If you take pride in your work, take the time to learn the right way to take accurate messages.

Nothing is more frustrating than missing a lucrative business opportunity because of sloppy handwriting, lost notes, late notices, name misspellings, wrong numbers, or inaccurate messages. If it hasn't happened to you yet, it soon will—unless you take steps.

Some companies set up brief training programs for employees, teaching them how to record phone messages with role-playing sessions and other techniques. Such a training program should work with a small group at a time and should be set up in an isolated area, where business will not be disrupted. One or two hours of practice is often enough for newcomers to grasp the principles.

If you substitute your own name and that of your firm for the ones shown, the following dialogues should help you and your employees practice your message-taking skills.

Employee: **"Telestar Inc., this is Wayne Smalley. May I help you?"**

Caller: "Hi, may I speak with Lana Plummer, please?"

Employee: "Who's calling please?"

Caller: "This is Dan Sparks. Is Lana there?"

Employee: "She's not in right now, Mr. Sparks. Would you like to leave a message?"

Caller: "Yes, would you please ask her to give me a call when she returns?"

Employee: "Ok, Mr. Sparks. Is that spelled s-p-a-r-k-s?"

Caller: "Yes, that's correct."

Employee: "And will she know what company you're with, Mr. Sparks?"

Caller: "I'm with the XYZ Company."

Employee: "Yes, Sir, the XYZ Company. And the number where you may be reached?"

Caller: "She can call me at area code 222, and the number is 555-2323."

Employee: "All right, that's area code 222, 555-2323. And is there an extension number?"

Caller: "Yes, I'm at extension 33."

Employee: "Extension 33. And did you wish to leave a message, Mr. Sparks?"

Caller: "Just tell her I have some information about the Hay-Long Project, and ask her to call me when she can."

Employee: "Yes, Sir. Is that spelled H-A-Y, L-O-N-G?"

Caller: "That's correct, with a hyphen."

Employee: "Ok. I'll tell her you have that information. And when is the best time for her to call you back, Mr. Sparks?"

Caller: "Oh, anytime before five o'clock is fine."

Employee: "If that's not possible, is there another number where you can be reached later?"

Caller: "Yes, she can call me this evening on my mobile phone at the same area code, 555-3838 if that's more convenient."

Employee: "Ok. That alternate number is also area code 222, 555-3838. When would be the best time for her to call at this alternate number, Mr. Sparks?"

Caller: "I'll be at that number between six and eight o'clock tonight."

Employee: "Between six and eight tonight. Let me read this back to you to be sure I have it right for Ms. Plummer. That's *Mr. Dan Sparks with the XYZ Company, and you have information for her about the Hay-Long Project. She can call you at 222, 555-2323, extension 33 before five P.M., or at 222, 555-3838 between six and eight o'clock tonight.* Is there anything else you'd like for me to tell her, Mr. Sparks?"

Caller: "No, you've got it exactly right. Thank you very much."

Employee: "It was a pleasure, Mr. Sparks, and thank you for calling Telestar Inc."

If a caller says the party he or she is trying to reach already has the phone number, be cautious. If the caller is a friend or client who calls often or a family member, accept the statement. Otherwise, ask for the number anyway.

Operator: "Could you give me that number again please, just in case he doesn't have it with him when he gets the message?"

Role playing is by far the fastest and most reliable way to teach employees how to take accurate messages. Use your own words of course, but try not to change the structure of these dialogues. You want your people to form the habit of using questions to control conversations.

Asking for the best time to return a call and an alternate number (or time) is the best way to avoid "telephone tag."

This is a good rule to follow religiously, a time-saver for everyone involved. Alternate times and phone numbers often eliminate the need for immediate replies and virtually ensure that both parties will connect eventually. No calling back to find out that now it's the other party who is out.

Message pads can improve accuracy.

There are a number of message pads you may purchase in office supply stores which can be useful for teaching anyone to take accurate messages. If you can't find one that fits your needs, make up your own and photocopy it, or have a supply specially printed. Or try the Instant Influence Message Memo shown in Figure 3:

Record the date and time of the call as well as the name of whoever took the message ("by"). Show for whom the message was taken and write in the caller's name and company in spaces provided. If the caller says he or she will call back, all you have to do is check the appropriate selection. Otherwise check "Please call" and write in the area code (if long distance), phone number, and extension (if any). Space is also provided for recording the best time for returning the call as well as an alternate phone number and time, too. Use the bottom portion of the Message Memo to write down the caller's message or any impressions or notes from the person taking the call. "Messenger checklist on back completed?——" is a quality control device we'll discuss shortly.

Message forms like the one shown here can act as an outline, to ensure that whoever answers your phone asks all pertinent questions in the proper order, and writes down the answers correctly. Just remember to . . .

Repeat important information out loud to the caller as you write it down. Be as legible as possible to insure accuracy.

After hanging up review each message to ensure that it is accurate and easy to read. A message that looks like a doctor's prescription is worthless. If your hasty handwriting comes out in a scrawl, rewrite the entire message as neatly as you can before you post it. Don't forget to post it promptly (after checking the appropriate space at the bottom confirming that you have completed The Messenger Checklist).

Shown in Figure 4, the Messenger Checklist (which should be printed on the reverse side of the Message Memo) includes six questions designed to help those using the Message Memo to review their messages to ensure accuracy and improve their skills.

If you can check all six questions on the Messenger Checklist, you did a fine job. If you missed any points, checking them will help you do it better the next time. If you work together, everyone

FIGURE 3: **INSTANT INFLUENCE MESSAGE MEMO**

DATE _____ TIME _____ A.M./P.M. BY _____

MESSAGE FOR: _____

CALLER'S NAME _____

COMPANY _____

( ) PLEASE CALL   ( ) WILL CALL BACK

1ST PHONE # ( ) _____ – _____ EXT ____

     WHEN: _____

2ND PHONE # ( ) _____ – _____ EXT ____

     WHEN: _____

MESSAGE / NOTES:

MESSENGER CHECKLIST ON BACK COMPLETED? _____

FIGURE 4: **INSTANT INFLUENCE MESSENGER CHECKLIST**

_____ 1. Were you prepared to process accurate messages quickly?

_____ 2. Did you repeat information out loud as you wrote it down?

_____ 3. Did you ask for alternate times and phone numbers to avoid "phone tag"?

_____ 4. Did you confirm spelling of caller's name, correct phone numbers, and accuracy of the message with caller before hanging up the phone?

_____ 5. Did you check your handwriting to be sure the person for whom the message is intended can read it?

_____ 6. Did you immediately post this message in a place where the person called will receive it quickly?

in your firm can use the Message Memo with the Messenger Checklist to improve their skills and quickly develop an efficient, reliable message system that is virtually fail-safe.

Priority No. 10: Maintain a Cheerful Composure at All Times.

Your cheerful attitude will be remembered, particularly if you keep smiling as you speak. This kind of Telestyle can establish the tone for the conversation that follows—even when you are just taking a message or routing the call to someone else. The ultimate recipient of the call will appreciate your setting the stage in a pleasant manner, and the caller will enjoy doing business with your firm.

Don't let a rude or indignant caller cause you to adopt the same bad attitude.

Be professional. Don't stoop to the level of those who cannot control their emotions. It is often difficult to maintain your cheerful composure when the caller is ranting at you, but responding in kind only makes things worse. Remain pleasant and helpful, and you have a good chance of turning the caller's mood around.

Control your mental attitude to keep it positive, and you will project a better professional image for your employer. You'll also enjoy your work a lot more.

Paying attention to priorities will help you maintain a cheerful composure and immediately take charge of all your incoming calls. The Top Ten Priorities for Answering Business Phones (hereafter referred to as the Top Ten) are summarized in Figure 5.

Review this list as often as you like to be sure you are giving your best efforts when answering your phones. Individually the Top Ten may not look all that impressive, but when used together, they have a subtle but very powerful impact upon callers. If you make a habit of remembering them all, you will become a great public relations representative for your firm every time you take a call.

If you are a receptionist or switchboard operator, these ten

FIGURE 5: **TOP TEN PRIORITIES FOR ANSWERING BUSINESS PHONES**

1. Answer your business calls on the first or second ring.

2. Create a positive first impression with a smiling Telestyle.

3. Use a prepared introduction when answering your business phone.

4. Identify the caller and repeat the name as soon as it is given.

5. Be a model of proper etiquette and courtesy.

6. Determine the purpose of the call as it relates to you.

7. Respect the value of the caller's time.

8. Use friendly questions to establish and maintain control of the conversation.

9. Be prepared to process accurate messages fast.

10. Maintain a cheerful composure at all times.

priorities will help you become more professional at your craft, and worth your weight in gold to your employer, too. If you are an entrepreneur just starting out, practice the Top Ten consistently. They will help you create a dynamic first impression with many clients whom you may meet only on the telephone.

Owners and managers will find that the better impression their employees make on the phone, the more customers and clients they will be able to attract. The Top Ten can help any executive or employee set the stage for handling his incoming calls more profitably. Remember . . .

The better the first impression you make, the faster you will be able to take charge of the conversation with questions. The faster you establish control of the conversation, the easier it will be to influence the outcome in your favor.

I guess the real magic of *Phone Tactics for Instant Influence* is that when you implement them correctly . . .

Most callers will never notice that you seized control of the conversation, nor how you did it. But they will remember talking with you as a pleasant experience.

3

WHEN TO USE INSTANT INFLUENCE WITH CALLS TO YOUR HOME

W e seldom feel the need to take charge of the calls we receive from friends and relatives, but what about calls from strangers? Most of us get calls at home from telephone solicitors, trying to sell something or seeking donations for schools, churches, and charitable organizations. How do you know which are reputable and which are not? How do you protect yourself from annoyance calls and criminals? What information about your family would your children divulge to strangers on the phone? What can you teach them?

Phone Tactics for Home Security

Anyone with your phone number can call you at any time of day or night. Although there is a way to "block" calls (which we'll discuss later) . . .

The telephone is the only entrance to your home that cannot be locked.

We need to know how to defend our homes from strangers. Burglars often call first to make sure the coast is clear before attempting a break-in. Rapists have been known to use a phone call to determine if a woman is alone. Kidnappers and child molesters have also used the same tactics.

No, I am not trying to scare you or cause undue concern, but if we don't take home security seriously, who will? One of the best ways to protect yourself from potential problems is to be very careful about the information you give out to strangers—beginning with the way you answer the phone when it rings. Some families seem to believe they sound more professional or dignified by answering the phone with an identifying statement like "Jones residence," etc. Others try to save time with wrong number calls by answering with their phone numbers: "This is 555–1203" or just "1203." Why give out information when you don't need to?

What's wrong with "hello"?

If you don't use your home for business, a simple "Hello?" or "Yes?" is by far the safest and most practical way to answer your phone, because it allows you to find out who is calling before you divulge any information. Regardless of how you answer the phone at home, the most important rule to follow for safety is this:

Identify callers before answering questions.

This basic rule of home security is particularly applicable where children and women are at home alone. It is also the one we tend to forget most often. A typical example of this is as follows.

Caller: "Is Jim there?
Wife: "No, he's in Atlanta on a business trip."

The wife in the above example has just told the caller that her husband is out of town without even knowing to whom she is speaking. Here is a situation where it is better to follow the Politician's Ploy and answer a question with a question . . .

Caller: "Is Jim there?"

Wife: "Who's calling, please?"

Caller: "This is Bill Thomas. May I speak to Jim?"

Wife: "I'm sorry, Bill, but I don't recognize your name. Does my husband know you?"

Caller "Oh yes, we met at a business lunch last week."

Wife (still not sure): "Well, he can't come to the phone right now. What number are you calling from?"

See how easy it is to seize control of a conversation with questions? Granted the wife in this example may sound a little evasive, but at least she has not put herself in an unsafe position by telling the caller she is alone. If the husband knows the caller, he can always explain her precautions when returning the call. Most people appreciate caution nowadays.

"Who's calling?", "Does he know you?", and "What number were you calling?"

are always good questions for women alone to ask. Children who are at home alone should be taught to say **"He (She) can't come to the phone right now,"** instead of telling callers that their parents are out, at work, or at the store. Friends will understand your caution, while those with ulterior motives will be foiled in their attempts to obtain information.

Teach your spouse and children how to control telephone conversations with questions. They will be safer and probably end up taking better messages, too.

There are two occasions when using questions to control a telephone conversation is *not* appropriate. The most obvious is a personal call between friends or relatives. The other may surprise you.

Annoyance calls should be ignored.

If you try to control a prank call or ask questions of someone who is being obscene or threatening on the telephone, you play right into the hands of the caller.

Annoyance callers thrive on reaction.

Immature, sick, or mentally disturbed—annoyance callers want you to be shocked, afraid, angry, or indignant. Your expressions of outrage would be a turn-on for the typical annoyance caller. Don't give him the satisfaction of any reaction at all.

If you receive an annoyance call, simply lay the phone down quietly without saying a word, <u>leave it off the hook</u>, and walk away.

Cover the receiver with a pillow if you have to remain in the same room, but *don't shout, slam down the receiver,* or *say anything to the caller at all.* Just leave it off the hook for fifteen to thirty minutes, and go next door to report the call to the phone company on a neighbor's phone. The caller will soon get bored, and since he or she cannot call you back, will probably try someone else. If he or she does call again, simply state (without showing emotion) that you do not wish to be called again, follow the procedure described above, and . . .

Write down an accurate record of the dates and times you received each annoyance call.

Without evidence, there is very little the police or telephone companies can do about annoyance calls, since it is difficult to identify such people or prove who used a particular phone, even when the number is known. Once a source phone is located, a written log of the dates and times you received each annoyance call will give phone company or law enforcement officials a way of identifying the caller.

Please understand that there are no foolproof tactics for dealing with annoyance calls, but the above one seems to be the best. To repeat: Lay the receiver down quietly and walk away, so that the caller gets bored talking to himself. Meanwhile, make a record of the date and time of the call, and report it to the phone company. If the phone number is listed in a female name, change the listing to your initials, and if the calls persist, get an unlisted number. Be very careful to whom you give your new number; if the calls continue, the caller is someone you know.

Remember these rules:

Show no emotion whatsoever. Always report such calls, with the dates and times of their occurrence, to your local phone company, and follow their instructions carefully.

Phone company officials are professionals and will have a good working relationship with the local police. Sadly enough, most police departments don't treat annoyance calls very seriously, since they are usually classed as misdemeanors instead of felonies. It may therefore be necessary to follow up several times with the local police and phone company, to ensure that your case gets the attention you want.

Help is on the way.

New Jersey and a handful of other states are experimenting with Atlantic Bell's Caller ID, a new invention that may help put a stop to repeated obscene phone calls and other annoyance calls. Caller ID is a boxlike device the phone company attaches to your phone (for an installation fee of around $100 plus rental of $10 to $20 per month). When your phone rings, Caller ID automatically displays the phone number of the caller trying to reach you.

Now, if you have Caller ID, you can identify the caller before you pick up the phone (if you recognize the number). If you don't wish to answer, you can "block" the call instead. You can even program this device to block all calls from a particular number in the future—a trouble making neighbor, for example, or a harassing ex-spouse. Instead of reaching you, callers hear a recorded message from the phone company stating that your phone has been programmed to block the call.

The applications (good and bad) for such a device are vast. No longer will police have to keep the caller on the phone several minutes to trace a call, because the caller's number is displayed immediately. Caller ID makes it a simple matter to identify which phones annoyance callers are using, and then to block those calls to your phone afterwards. You will have something concrete to report to the police, too.

Exercise caution with wrong-number calls.

Most wrong-number calls are as innocent as they seem—a careless misdialing. But this is also a common ruse for burglars. Some place a call first to see if anyone is at home, and use the excuse of a wrong number if the phone is answered. A few just hang up, but others will ask for a fictitious person or try to obtain information. Those asking questions are the ones you should be particularly leery of. Below are some typical questions along with responses that will help you protect your home security:

Caller: "Is Joe there?"

Response: "No, there's no one here by that name. What number were you calling?"

Caller: "Hey, who's this?"

Response: "Excuse me, who were you calling?"

Caller: "What number is this?"

Response: "What number were you calling?"

These responses sound evasive, but what if they do? They help you avoid divulging information to the wrong people. Legitimate wrong number callers seldom waste time with a lot of questions once they know they've reached the wrong number. If you and your family practice controlling conversations with questions and avoid giving out information to strangers, you will have done about as much as any family can to protect your telephone security at home.

Special Precautions for Single Women

All the precautions and tactics we've discussed so far are doubly applicable to women who live alone. Although most of us are aware of the ploy, it still makes more sense for single women to have their phones listed under their initials instead of their given names. Every woman should be proud of her sex, but why advertise the fact in the local phone book? Initials are safer.

Occasionally single women get a call from someone asking to speak with her husband or with Mr. So-and-so (her last name). Most are telephone solicitors who are instructed to speak with husbands first, but this may also be a ruse used by rapists and obscene callers. Since it is virtually impossible to tell the difference at first, single women would be wise to employ precautionary Teletactics. Remember, if you are single (and not recently widowed, divorced, or separated) . . .

Friends and people who know you will not ask for your husband.

If you receive such a call, don't divulge any information to a stranger or tell the caller that you are single. Handle it this way.

Woman: "Hello?"

Caller: "May I speak with your husband, please?"

Woman: "He can't come to the phone right now. May I ask who's calling?"

Caller: "This is Joe, is your husband in?"

Woman: "I don't recognize your name, Joe. Are you sure you have the right number?"

Caller: "I was calling Jim Thomas."

Woman: "Well, that's not my husband's name. I'm afraid you've got the wrong number."

Notice that the woman in the above example never indicated that she was single, alone, or that her "husband" was not at home? As stated earlier, most of these calls are honest mistakes, but why take chances?

Most single women will occasionally get calls from men they know of only through friends, asking for a date. This is as it should be, and I would never suggest that one should curtail or limit one's social life by being overcautious. If the caller sounds nice or interesting, by all means make a blind date, but don't allow him to pick you up at your home on the first date. Arrange to meet him in a public place like a restaurant or club, where you have a chance to get to know him before allowing him to come into your home where you are alone.

> **Woman: "I have some errands to take care of first, so why don't I just meet you there at seven-thirty. Or would eight o'clock be better for you?"**

Use your own transportation to and from this first meeting place. A little caution is a lot safer, and these days "safer" means the same thing as "smarter."

A Considerate Way to Turn Down a Date

Some single people have a hard time turning down requests for dates from acquaintances they don't wish to hurt—or go out with either. Instead of saying "I like you but I'm not at all interested in spending my evenings alone with you," most people resort to a series of lame excuses that cause the caller to try again and again until the truth finally dawns.

Sure it's hard to say no to someone you'll see every day in class or at work, and you certainly don't want to say anything that might hurt his feelings. But why lead this person on to continue calling in the future? At least say something that shows him he should spend his time pursuing someone else. You can easily avoid lying or hurting a friend if you will make two promises to yourself right now: "I promise, first, not to go out with anyone I don't want to and, second, never to discuss this promise with anyone."

The next time you receive an unwelcome call for a date, you won't have to lie. Handle it this way:

> Caller: "Hi, this is Joe Baker from work. I just got two tickets to the Springsteen concert next Thursday night. Would you like to go with me?"

You: (regretfully) **"I'm sorry, Joe. I promised not to. But Alice Thompson loves Bruce Springsteen. Why not ask her?"**

Caller: "Well, I guess I could. What do you mean, you promised?"

You: **"I'm sorry, but I also promised never to discuss it with anyone. You wouldn't ask me to break my word, would you?"**

Caller: "No, but maybe some other time?"

You: **"No, I'm afraid not, but thanks for asking. I really do have to get off the phone now. Are you going to call Alice?"**

Caller: "I guess so. Well, take care . . ."

You: **"OK, and thanks again, Joe . . . 'bye."**

Sure, it sounds a little vague and mysterious, but this method does offer a way to be truthful and definitely say 'no' without saying something hurtful. Notice how the caller's concentration was diverted by the suggestion of someone else. If such a suggestion is phrased in the form of a question, it not only provides a distraction, but establishes and maintains control of the conversation, too.

If the caller is someone you definitely do not like and whose feelings you don't care about, just say something like . . .

Woman: "No, I'll never go out with you and will not discuss it. Can we just say good-bye and leave it at that?"

Brief and to the point, a definite statement like this should end the discussion without being insulting. I prefer the "promise" method because it is more courteous, but the direct method is sometimes necessary—particularly if you are dealing with a real jerk. However, save it for a last resort.

How to Teach Children to Take Messages

Most preschool children are simply too young to answer the phone without being a nuisance to the caller. Until they can write, they are not reliable message takers, either. If you want to take a chance on letting a toddler be "Mom or Dad's little helper" while you are present, teach him or her to say . . .

Child: "You'll have to talk to my mom (dad). Who's calling please?"

Show your children how to cover the mouthpiece with a hand before summoning you. Be sure they know that the receiver should be left off the hook when they run to get you. Teach them that it's not nice to listen in. If all this sounds too complicated, then your preschooler is not ready to answer the phone.

If your older children can write legibly and carry on an intelligent conversation, there is no reason why they cannot be taught how to answer the phone properly and take good messages. Make it easy for them by keeping a message or memo pad and a pencil by each phone in your home at all times. Establish one place in your home for posting messages. Forming the habit of always using the same message center is as good a rule to follow in your home as it is at work. Many families post messages on the refrigerator, using magnets. We use a box with slots for messages and keep it by the kitchen phone. It does not matter what spot you select, as long as you form the habit of posting messages in the same place every time.

The best way to teach children (as well as adults) to protect home security and take accurate messages is with role-playing sessions, similar to those recommended for business. These sessions can be fun for the kids, and help avoid problems or embarrassing headaches for you, too. Make role playing a game and offer a prize for doing it well. The following dialogues should help:

Child: "Hello?"
Caller: "Hi, may I speak to your dad please?"
Child: "Who's calling, please?"

Caller: "This is John Truitt."

Child: "OK, Mr. Truitt, can you hold please?"

Notice how the child in this example courteously repeats the last name of the caller with the appropriate "Mr." or "Ms." as soon as it is given? Courtesy makes a good impression, and as stated earlier, repeating the caller's name as soon as it is given helps whoever is taking a message remember it. If the parent is not at home or cannot come to the phone, continue this way.

Child: "He can't come to the phone right now, Mr. Truitt, but I can take a message. What number are you calling from?"

Caller: "Ask him to call me at 555–2334."

Child: "Yes, sir, your number is 555–2334, and would you spell your last name for me, please?"

Caller: "That's T-R-U-I-T-T, have you got that?"

Child: "Yes, sir, and is there a message, too?"

If there is a message, the youngster should write it down and read it back to the caller out loud to ensure accuracy.

Child: "When is the best time for him to call you back?"

Caller: "Oh anytime before five o'clock is fine."

Child: "If that's not possible, is there another number where you can be reached later?"

Caller: "Why yes, he can call me tonight at 555–3838 if that's more convenient."

Child: "OK, Mr. Truitt, that alternate number is 555–3838. When is the best time for him to call you there?"

Caller: "Any time between seven and ten PM will be fine."

Child: "Yes sir, Mr. Truitt. I'll give him the message."

If the caller persists in asking the parent's whereabouts . . .

Child: "I don't know what he's doing right now, but he asked me to answer the phone and take messages. Was there anything else you wanted me to tell him?"

Repeating the caller's name, phone number, and message (if any) out loud to the caller to ensure accuracy is just as important at home as it is at work. Asking for alternate phone numbers and times to return a call is also a good habit for anyone taking messages at home to form as well.

Children left alone should always be given a phone number where they may call their parents in an emergency.

Don't let your children give this number to strangers. Instead instruct them to call you and repeat the message over the phone, so you can answer it promptly if it's legitimate. This is a simple precautionary measure that ensures your children's safety and also prevents strangers from learning that they are at home alone.

Whether or not they are able to phone the parent, children should be taught to post the note immediately in the family message spot.

You and your family can have fun learning to take messages properly if you practice together. As suggested earlier, offer a prize (candy, movie tickets, dessert, etc.) for the child who uses the most cheerful Telestyle and seems quickest with the right response. Role playing with your children is also the best way to practice these techniques yourself. Be patient and practice longer with those who are slower to catch on, and you will all be winners in the end.

Business Calls at Home Require Accurate Messages

If you or your spouse get the kind of business calls at home that affect your income, job performance, or career success, then practice the dialogues for taking messages given in the previous chapter, except for changing your introduction as shown below:

Spouse: "Hello?"
Caller: "Hi, may I speak with Judy Thomas, please?"
Spouse: "Who's calling please?"
Caller: "This is John Truitt. Is Judy there?"
Spouse: "John, she can't come to the phone right now, but I'll

> **be glad to take a message for you. Is this a business or personal call?"**
>
> Caller: "It's a business call."
>
> **Spouse: "OK, and what company are you with?"**

Message forms like the Instant Influence Message Memo (Figure 3) can act as an outline for whoever answers your phone to ensure that all pertinent questions are asked in the proper order, and that the answers are written down correctly. The Messenger Checklist (Figure 4) makes it easy to improve your skills quickly. Although you need not professionalize your message taking with friends and relatives, these more frequent calls will help your family get in the habit of writing down phone messages and posting them in the same place every time.

Before You Put Someone on Hold . . .

If you have a "hold" feature on your home phone, be sure everyone in your family knows how to use it properly. Some home phone systems allow the phone answerer to hang up one instrument while the one being called picks up another. Others only work properly if the person called picks up the same instrument where the call was put on hold. In the latter case if the party called picks up an extension phone, that can result in a disconnection. If your hold feature is that temperamental, you would probably be better off covering the mouthpiece the old-fashioned way before asking the person called to pick up the phone.

Dealing with Telephone Solicitors

Many people consider all such calls a nuisance. However, many reputable companies, organizations, and salespeople regularly depend on telephone solicitation to contact people directly in their homes. The pros will use most of the skills described in this book very effectively. You can be just as skillful as they are with practice. You already have a big advantage over most telemarketers, because you can always say no, or "I'm not interested," and hang up the phone, ending the discussion.

Some of us may occasionally end up buying something we don't really need, but there is very little to fear from an honest salesperson. The true professionals enjoy their work, like and respect their customers, and take too much pride in their profession to lie. They want you to enjoy doing business with them, and they look forward to building the kind of relationship with their customers that generates more sales in the future.

Problems arise from the few bad apples—con men and pitch artists who hawk misrepresented merchandise and overpriced services to the naive and unsuspecting. Fortunately, such fly-by-night businesses usually have acquired a file of complaints with the local BBB (Better Business Bureau) or Chamber of Commerce, which you may easily check by phone. If you are solicited by phone by a representative of a company you have never heard of, *always* . . .

Ask for references and verify them. Then check with your local BBB or Chamber of Commerce before paying out money, agreeing to sign anything, divulging your credit card number, or buying anything.

I would go a step further and recommend that you even check out those businesses you *have* heard of, to be sure the specific offer you want to participate in has a clean bill of health.

Peace of mind is worth a few phone calls.

If you forget to check references before you buy, the FTC (Federal Trade Commission) has initiated a series of laws that may help save you from financial losses due to misrepresentation and other unscrupulous or deceptive sales practices.

Today Federal consumer protection laws allow a three day "cooling-off period."

Anyone who purchases something from a salesperson in his or her home is allowed three business days (excluding weekends and holidays) to reconsider the purchase. If you decide not to go through with the purchase, you can cancel the order for a full refund, with no questions asked and no strings attached.

Use these three days to compare prices, check with the local BBB, verify references, or have your lawyer review the contract or any other written agreement.

It is easy to identify unscrupulous salespeople because they all use some kind of gimmick or teaser to make you think you are getting something for nothing. Their phone pitch usually starts out with a statement like "Congratulations Mr. Jones, you have just won . . ." or "Your family has just been selected to receive, . . ." or "Yours is one of the few families in your neighborhood to qualify for a substantial discount. . . ."

If it sounds too good to be true, it probably is.

There is no such thing as something for nothing. Even legitimate contests with real prize winners require entrants to have some kind of winning ticket or at least to fill out an entry form. Anyone who calls you out of the blue to tell you that you've won a contest that you have not entered should be treated with a great deal of skepticism.

"Surveys" are also used as come-ons by some con artists. They'll ask you a few questions to see if you already have the product or service they are selling, or if you are financially able to buy. Legitimate researchers will always identify themselves and their organizations first. Most will explain the purpose of their survey and courteously ask if you have time to answer their questions. Few if any will pressure you for answers if you say you don't have the time. Those who do are probably salespeople instead of legitimate researchers.

The easiest way to defend yourself from pitch men and con artists without being rude to the legitimate salesperson, pollster, or researcher would be to handle the call like this:

Callee: "Thanks for calling, but we are really not interested. Can we just say good-bye?"

Most legitimate researchers and pollsters will honor your request. Salespeople and fund-raisers for charities will probably try a little harder to arouse your interest. If you think you might be interested in learning more about a salesperson's product or a fund-raiser's cause, ask the caller to send you some information in the mail. If the caller positively refuses to do this, he or she is probably not on the up and up. You're better off disengaging:

> **Callee: "I'm sorry but I don't want to talk about it at all. Can we hang up now?"**

This kind of definite statement should end the discussion. If not, just hang up the phone.

Some people are angered by all telephone solicitors, considering them an invasion of privacy. They get extremely agitated and shout at the caller, curse out him or her, and angrily slam down the receiver. I'm sure all of us, at one time or another, have dashed out of the shower to answer the phone and felt indignant when the caller turned out to be selling something or taking a survey. But why let it ruin your day? Often such callers are young people just starting out or working for very worthwhile causes that help the community. Just handle the call politely and get off the line.

I personally can't stand getting telephone calls from a machine— those irritating computers with recorded messages that some tele-marketing companies use to make their calls for them. The only person dumber than the one who listens to one of these calls is the one who purchased such a machine for his company in the first place. The scientist who invents a device to send an electrical charge back through the phone lines to blow up these machines would be making a real contribution to society. Until then, hanging up the phone will have to do.

Certain organizations today offer, as a service, to have your name and phone number removed from telemarketers' lists. This is probably not very effective, because new businesses are started all the time and new phone lists prepared. Others have suggested that consumers demand a payment for use of their private phone lines by telephone solicitors.

> **Callee: "If you'll agree to pay me $10 per minute for tying up my private phone and taking up my time, I'll be glad to**

listen to your pitch. First give me your name and address, so I'll know where to send the bill, and I'll get my timer. Does that sound fair enough to you?"

I guess this can work if you enjoy sparring with telephone solicitors, but I seriously doubt if you can collect on your bargain. If and when Caller ID becomes available in your area, you can use it to block sales calls from numbers you know, but not those first calls from solicitors who have never contacted you before.

The truth is that, in the future, more and more companies and individuals will be using the phone to save time doing everything. Short of disconnecting your home phone, changing it to an unlisted number (which may affect your credit rating), or moving to some small island near Tahiti, the best way to get along with this new phenomenon is to dismiss unwanted calls politely but firmly.

Make all your telephone conversations enjoyable.

No matter who I talk with on the telephone, I always enjoy the conversation more if I practice a friendly, cheerful Telestyle. Since people usually react in kind, my conversations are nearly all friendly. I feel good when I hang up the phone, and I like to think other people enjoy talking with me.

Keep Cool When Collection Agents Call

Financial experts across the country constantly advise consumers to notify their creditors in advance when they foresee problems with paying their bills, but it's human to stall and keep your fingers crossed. And pretty soon the phone is ringing and a collector is on the line. Anyone dealing with a collection call is at a decided disadvantage, but Teletactics like Truitt's Law, choices of two, and the Reverse can help you take charge of such conversations and gain the time and terms you need to work things out.

The first rule for handling this problem is . . .

Don't lie to bill collectors.

Don't say "the check is in the mail" if it isn't. Most collectors keep accurate records of their calls and the promises and statements made during their conversations. From the collector's point of view, the whole purpose of a collection call is to extract a promise to pay a specific amount by a specific date. Their goal of course is to bring your account up to date, but most (not all) will accept a partial payment, particularly if you have a history of honest dealings with them in the past. If they catch you lying, however, or failing to honor your promises, they will classify you as a deadbeat, and from then on they will harass you unmercifully.

The second rule for dealing with collectors on the phone is . . .

Don't make promises you can't keep.

This sounds easier than it really is. Remember, the purpose of a collection call is to obtain promises.

> Collector: "Listen Mr. Baker, we want a certified check to bring your account up to date in our office no later than one o'clock this Friday afternoon."

Reverse the intimidating effects of this kind of statement by making a counter offer: (1) Start with a statement of agreement. (2) Offer to send *half* the amount you think you can, *five days later* than your most pessimistic prediction of when you should have the money. (3) Use a choice of two to deflect the attention of the collector away from your terms toward ways of helping you resolve your problem with his or her superior.

> **Consumer: "I can certainly understand your concern, but in all honesty the most I could possibly send you is fifty dollars, and I couldn't even do that before the twenty-first. I know it's not much, but that's the only promise I can honestly make at this time. Do you have the authority to accept it, or do you need to check with someone else?"**
>
> Collector: "When would you be able to pay the rest, Mr. Baker?"
>
> **Consumer: I honestly can't promise you any more than I've**

said right now. However I _am_ going to bring my account up to date as soon as I possibly can. I will notify you when I know more. Is that fair enough?"

Collector: "No sir, that's not good enough. I have to have a payment by Friday afternoon at the latest."

Consumer: "I know you're good at your job, but I've told you all I can do. Would you rather have nothing at all, or would you like to present my offer to your supervisor and call me back?"

Quite frankly the reason I say promise to send half what you think you can send five days later than you think you can send it is because of other problems you may be facing at the same time. When things are going badly, chances are that more than one collector is calling or will be shortly. Promising _less later_ may help you avoid having to break your promise if things don't go as planned. If you come up with more money sooner, your creditor will happily accept it. In fact, he'll think a lot more of you than if you had simply kept a promise to send more by the earlier date.

If you keep a friendly attitude, you'll be cool enough to use the Teletactics you need to get collectors on your side. All most of them want is to move your file out of the "past due" box and back into their "current accounts." Most collectors will cooperate with you _if they believe you are being honest and sincere with them._ Although it may take time, bringing your account up to date voluntarily is still faster and cheaper for both you and your creditor than legal action.

However, there are a few collectors who don't even deserve a minute of your time.

No bill collector has the right to be rude, threatening, or insulting.

Don't waste your valuable time with louts. If a collector crosses the line of propriety and uses vulgar language, threats, or screaming insults, handle the call as you would any other obscene caller: Lay the phone down, leave it off the hook for a while—and then call your lawyer.

Most states have laws to protect debtors from unscrupulous or obscene collection agents and late-night or on-the-job harassment calls. Since these laws vary with the fifty states, ask your lawyer or local Consumer Credit Counseling Service about the statutes in your area and your recourses against agents who violate them. Don't overreact to the statements of bill collectors. If you consider the problems you've solved before, you will realize that you will solve your credit problems, too.

Focus your attention beyond your problems, on solutions.

If a collector starts giving you a hard time on the phone, look beyond his intimidating methods and remember the Teletactics you need to influence the call in your favor.

Handling Responses to Your "For Sale by Owner" Ads

Whether you are selling a piece of jewelry, a house, a car, or a baby bed, the purpose of running a "For Sale by Owner" ad is to attract the best prospects to purchase the item you are offering for sale. A few basic strategies and Teletactics used by sales professionals will help you answer the calls better and induce more respondents to come see the merchandise. Before planning the sale, ask yourself the following questions about legalities:

1. What (if any) local, state, or federal laws apply to the sale you are contemplating?
2. Will you need special forms for vehicle registration, title and transfer, a bill of sale, earnest money contract, collecting sales tax, etc.?
3. Will you need to show proof of ownership, clear title, sales slips, service records, breeding documents, etc.?

If you don't know the answers to these three questions, ask your attorney, state and local tax collectors, or the IRS office. Now think about the item itself. How will you sell it? What will you say about it? Get out a legal pad or note pad and write out your answers to the following questions so you will have notes to help you plan the sale.

1. Describe the item(s) you wish to sell.
2. What different types of people will be most likely to buy it?
3. List five reasons the right prospect will buy it.
4. What's it worth?
5. Lowest price you will accept in cash?
6. Will you have to deliver it? Cost involved? How much (if any) would you discount the price if buyer handled delivery?
7. Will you have to make repairs or offer any kind of warranty? Cost involved? How much (if any) would you discount the sale price if sold "as is"?
8. How will you show it? Is cleanup necessary to make it look good? Cost involved?
9. What can you offer (discount, terms, warranty, free delivery, etc.) to help close the sale?
10. Will you need to make credit arrangements, use a promissory note, accept checks, or cash only?
11. List three reasons you purchased the item in the first place, three ways it has served you well, and discuss why you want to sell it.
12. Who will answer the calls?
13. Will those answering calls be able to answer questions about the item(s) for sale and give good directions for finding your home? (Write out directions that may be read over the phone.)
14. Should your address be printed in the ad?
15. Should special hours for calling appear in the ad?
16. When are the best times on your family's schedule to have prospects come to your home?
17. Should someone else be there for security?
18. Should a log be kept of your calls?

Although question 1 is self-explanatory, write a description of the item(s) for sale in the most flattering but truthful terms you can. This exercise should help you develop some good selling points and write an attractive ad, too. Question 2 will help you write the ad to appeal to the most likely prospects, and may also help you determine the best publication to advertise in to reach the type of prospects you want.

Along with 1, question 3 will give you more selling points you can use to talk about on the phone or when showing the item for sale. Questions 4 through 8 will help you determine a fair price to charge, while 9 and 10 should help you think of more ways to close and handle the financial part of the sale as well. Your answers to number 11 will not only provide additional selling points, they may even give you the extra ammunition you need to close the sale with a hesitant prospect. Use questions 12–17 to plan your schedule for answering calls and showing whatever you are selling to prospects.

Most families will answer yes to 18, so they will have a record of callers' names, phone numbers, and appointments. A log helps them to plan their schedules for showing, or to cancel later appointments after the item is sold. Draw vertical dividing lines in a notebook or on a legal pad to create spaces for listing the *date* of the response, *name* and *phone number* of the caller, and *day* and *time* you set an appointment for viewing your sale item. Leave a little space to the side for recording any comments like price quoted over the phone, etc. If you use a legal pad you will have enough horizontal lines to list about twenty to twenty-five callers to the page.

After answering all of the above questions and adding up the costs involved (including the price of an ad) you may wish to consider one other question:

Do you really need to sell the item, or would you be better off donating it to charity for a tax deduction? If so, be sure you don't "overvalue" the item and become liable for tax penalties and interest.

The person who wants to handle the sale himself has to begin thinking like a sales pro. If you want to sell something (anything), you have to become a want creator. That's what selling is— making the prospect want whatever you're talking about. It helps of course to have a salable product, but the best way to make anyone want anything is to get excited when you show or describe it.

Nothing sells like enthusiasm.

We've already discussed how you can raise the volume and speed of your voice to sound enthusiastic on the telephone. This technique is particularly important for handling responses to your "For Sale by Owner" ad. Answer the phone with a cheerful, enthusiastic Telestyle, encouraging the prospect to come over and see the item for sale.

Don't try to sell it over the telephone. Rarely will used items in "For Sale by Owner" ads be purchased sight unseen over the telephone. Selling is a step-by-step procedure.

First: Make the prospect want to see your product.
Second: Make the prospect want to own it.
Third: Help the prospect buy it.

Your first priority is to get prospects to come to your home and see the item or items for themselves. Naturally, the more prospects who see it, the more likely you are to sell it. Write out a brief script that uses forced-response questions to set up appointments with as many callers as possible, and keep a copy of directions for finding your home with your appointment log by the phone. The following sample dialogues will demonstrate how you can combine questions with Truitt's Law to control conversations, and use a choice of two for setting appointments:

Seller: "Hello?"

Caller: "I'm calling about the '74 Dodge you advertised in the paper for $1500. It is in good condition?"

Seller: "Oh, yes. Who's calling please?"

Caller: "This is Bill Jacobs. How many miles on that old Dodge anyway?"

Seller: "It's only got 68,000 miles on it, Bill. Would you like to set up a time to drive it yourself this afternoon, or would tonight be more convenient for you?"

Caller: "Oh I couldn't come tonight. Could we try it tomorrow?"

Seller: "Sure, whichever is best—morning or early afternoon?"

Notice how the seller answered the caller's questions, but finished his answer with a forced-response question to regain control of the conversation and focus upon the best time to see the car. Watch how he continues to offer choices of two until he has arranged a definite appointment.

> **Seller: "Great, you want to say 1 P.M. tomorrow or would 1:30 give you more time to get here?"**
>
> Caller: "1:30 sounds fine. Can you give me directions for finding your house?"
>
> **Seller: "Sure, Bill. I'll write down your name for 1:30 tomorrow. Could you give me your phone number in case we have to call you to reschedule?"**
>
> Caller: "OK, my number is 555–3213. Can you give me those directions now?"
>
> **Seller: "I'll be glad to. Do you have a pen and paper?"**

Most people who respond to your "For Sale by Owner" ad will have several questions prepared in order to save their time and find out more about your item before coming out to see it. "How much is it?" "What kind of condition is it in?" "Will you accept a personal check?" "Will you deliver?" These are all examples of the types of questions you may expect to hear from callers. Write out the questions you would ask if you were a buyer and plan your answers beforehand. Follow Truitt's Law by attaching questions of your own to the end of your answers so you can turn more of those inquiries into appointments.

> **Callee: "Oh, yes, it's a beautiful home, but you really need to walk through it yourself. Could you and your husband run by and see it tomorrow, or would later in the week be more convenient for you?"**
>
> **"Sure we can deliver, or make it worth your while to do it yourself. Can you drop by and see it this afternoon, or would tomorrow morning be better for you?"**

> "Yes, he's had all his shots, and we've got all his papers. Would you like to bring your little girl around to see him tonight, or would tomorrow after school be better?"

If you cannot answer the caller's questions set up an appointment for the caller to meet with the person in your family who is more knowledgable about the item you are offering for sale:

Callee: "I'm sorry, I don't know the answer to that, but someone who knows all about it will be here tomorrow afternoon to answer all your questions. Can you come to see it then, or would Wednesday be more convenient for you?"

One point to remember when using a choice of two:

Make sure both the times you suggest are convenient for you and your family before you suggest them.

If you plan your answers to the most probable questions in advance and handle the unexpected with Truitt's Law or the Politician's Ploy, you'll be ready for anything. Smile, speak with enthusiasm, and keep your end of the conversation focused upon arranging the appointment, and you will have a lot of prospects.

Once the prospect arrives, go over your selling points *enthusiastically* while demonstrating or showing the item you are offering for sale, and ask the prospect if he or she would really like to own it. Keep showing it this way until you find the prospect who wants it and believes the price is affordable. Then accept his or her money and close with a handshake.

Honesty keeps you out of trouble, and your enthusiasm will influence the right prospect to want to buy from you.

You will not only sell the item(s) you want to sell quickly, but you'll also sleep better afterward. Both you and the buyer will be glad you did business together.

Phone Tips for a Business in the Home

Many people who work at home have a separate phone line installed in the name of the business. Others use the same phone number for both their business and private lines. The advantages of separate lines probably outweigh those of the single line for privacy, tax purposes, and advertising. Two phone lines also make it easier to determine whether a call is for your business or residence before answering.

On the other hand one line is cheaper than two and often more convenient, since you can pick up a business call on every extension phone in your home. Moreover, separate phones can really be a hassle when both start ringing at the same time, and you are the only person around to answer them, too.

If you have a separate phone line in your home for business, answer that phone with the name of your firm. If you use your residence phone number for business calls too, however, you may want to answer your phone by simply giving your name:

Callee: "This is John Truitt."

Anyone calling another member of your family will ask for whoever he or she wishes to speak with anyway. Those calling you for business will assume they've gotten your private office and go ahead with the discussion. In any event, don't allow any phone used for business to ring too long without picking it up.

Business calls are your source of income.

The Top Ten priorities discussed in Chapter 2 will help make your home-based business as successful as one using commercial space.

Should You Use an Answering Service or Machine?

Anyone liable to be called in an emergency—not only doctors but plumbers, volunteer firemen, oil delivery services, and so on—

should have an answering service. But a machine may be more practical if all you need is a message taker while you are out on an errand. What counts is the type of business you are in. Patients may need to contact the doctor in off hours. A writer may need to leave his calls to the message machine while he concentrates on the undoing of his villain.

If you are frequently away from the phone during normal business hours, an answering service with friendly, cheerful operators will make a much better impression on callers than will a machine. On the other hand, unless you purchase something very sophisticated, most machines are considerably less expensive than answering services. I don't like machines but I have to concede that they have their uses. Only you can decide whether the personal touch provided by an answering service is worth the added costs to your business.

What Kind of Message to Use on Your Answering Machine

I would not even attempt to recommend one brand of answering machine or automated message system over another because new ones are being introduced all the time. Today some computer software programs allow your personal computer to answer your phone. All commonly used answering machines allow you to prerecord a message. After a predetermined number of rings, the machine answers your phone and automatically plays back the message. The good ones allow you to check messages by remote control; you just dial your home number from any Touch-Tone phone by punching in code numbers after dialing the machine. Others require the use of a special remote control device. Most machines allow the caller to enter a brief message after a "beep" that indicates when the machine is ready to record. Some models are voice-activated and have no beep sound.

Computer software packages work essentially the same way, except that messages are recorded on computer chips or storage disks instead of tape. They also allow you to leave specific messages for different callers, who enter certain prearranged code numbers through a Touch-Tone phone. Some may even be preprogrammed to perform a variety of other tasks, including calling you at another number to relay messages immediately. Regardless of the sophistication of the equipment you use, be sure your message is clear and easily understood, and does not act as an invitation to burglars by divulging that you and your family are away on vacation for two weeks.

Whether you use a computer or recorder type of answering device, keep the message as simple as possible, and more people will respond by leaving messages on it. Whether you use your home phone for business or private use only, the following sample message should be all you need to say:

> **Recording: "I'm sorry we can't take your call right now; wait until you hear the sound of the tone to state your name and phone number, the date and time you called, and a brief message . . . we'll get back to you as soon possible."**

This message protects home security by not giving out any information a burglar can use. It should be suitable for anyone, because it does not indicate whether the caller has reached a business or residence phone. Business callers and friends alike will simply leave a message. Knowing the dates and times people called can be a big help if you expect twenty or thirty messages. When recording your message, smile to make your voice sound pleasant and speak clearly. Use enthusiasm to add life to your message, and don't forget to mention the beep if your machine uses one. Once you have recorded a satisfactory message for your machine, leave it alone. Impulsive changes might inadvertently admit information that would reveal how long you intend to stay away.

Many people are still irritated by answering machines, but most of us have become resigned to them by now. After all, they are an improvement over an unanswered phone. Answering machines can help ensure that you don't miss important calls while you are away or unable to answer your phone. If you form the habit of checking your messages regularly and returning calls quickly, friends and business associates will not mind leaving messages on your answering machine.

Be Prepared for Emergency Calls

It is to be hoped that you will never receive a late-night call from an Emergency Room asking for critical medical data about a family member. What would happen if such a call came in while you were away, and only a neighbor, babysitter, or one of your children were there to receive it? There are no quick answers or Teletactics for handling emergency calls; there is just preparation. Figure 6 is an Emergency Data Sheet. Fill it out now, and it may well save vital minutes when a life is at stake.

With good luck, you will never need it, but take the time to fill out the Emergency Data Sheet as legibly as you can. Most of the spaces are self-explanatory. If you have 911 Emergency Service in your area, that is the only phone number you will need to fill in at the top for "Police, Fire and Ambulance." 911 operators also have a way of determining the address where an emergency phone call originated, but it saves priceless time if all pertinent information is kept beside the phone: address, cross streets, landmarks, neighbors' phone numbers, doctor's phone number, and medical data about your family. Neighbors, babysitters, or visitors may be the only people available in a pinch.

Make extra copies of your completed Emergency Data Sheet and post one near every phone in your home. Make sure that it is prominently displayed near the most used phone (usually in the kitchen) where others can readily find it.

Both you and your spouse should also keep a copy of a completed Emergency Data Sheet in your purse or wallet for emergencies that occur when you're at work, away from home, or on a trip. Rather than waste precious time when every second counts, you or someone else can read off critical data a lot faster if you have it written down in advance. It can also help the user provide accurate data in panic situations where emotions are hard to control, and it is

FIGURE 6: **EMERGENCY DATA SHEET**

POLICE: _____ FIRE: _____ AMBULANCE: _____

POISON CONTROL CENTER: _____ OTHER: _____ / _____

RESIDENCE OF: _____ PHONE: _____

STREET ADDRESS: _____

DIRECTIONS FOR LOCATING: _____

_____

_____

NEIGHBOR'S NAME: _____ PHONE: _____ HOUSE NO.: ____

DATA ON RESIDENTS & FAMILY MEMBERS:

NAME	AGE	DAY PHONE	BLOOD TYPE	PHYSICIAN	PHONE	SPECIAL MEDICATION OR INFO
____	___	____	____	_____	____	_____
____	___	____	____	_____	____	_____
____	___	____	____	_____	____	_____
____	___	____	____	_____	____	_____
____	___	____	____	_____	____	_____
____	___	____	____	_____	____	_____

NOTIFY IN EMERGENCY: _____ PHONE: _____

RELATIONSHIP: _____ ADDRESS: _____

NOTES: _____

_____

difficult to even think rationally (particularly if you are injured or incapacitated). Although I sincerely hope you never need to provide such information in an emergency, the time you save by having it written down in advance may indeed help save the life of someone dear to you.

4

INFLUENCE
INCOMING CALLS
FOR PROFIT
AND PRODUCTIVITY

The best way to use INSTANT INFLUENCE with incoming calls is in sales, because you can see immediate, tangible results in increased revenues. The telephone gives your customers and prospects instant access to your firm. There is no better tool for answering inquiries, qualifying prospects, arranging presentations, increasing orders, and even closing certain kinds of sales and business deals quickly.

More and more businesses have expanded their markets considerably by means of toll-free 800 numbers, advertising them in direct mail, print media, billboards, radio and television commercials. Computers, credit cards and toll free phone numbers are rapidly turning most if not all the old mail-order houses into telemarketing centers. We even have Home Shopping Clubs on television, selling a variety of consumer goods by telephone twenty-four hours a day.

Anytime you have your phone number printed on your business cards, letterheads, brochures, and other promotional materials, you're inviting customers and prospects to place orders by telephone or call for information. Although the number and types of callers may depend upon the kinds of products or services you sell, there are basically three types of prospects who will call your firm:

Type 1: Those who have already decided to buy from you.
Type 2: Those who must be sold face to face, or in two or more meetings or telephone conversations.
Type 3: Those who might be persuaded on the phone to buy during the first call.

The first type of prospect may already be a customer, calling in a new order or reorder. Those answering direct-response ads or phoning in their orders from your catalog would also fit into this category. Type 1 telephone orders are by far the easiest to handle, although the real profit potential lies in your ability to increase the amount of the order with better phone skills.

The second type of prospect usually involves a large purchase or a complex service, and probably needs to be sold face to face, in order that all key decision makers can be brought together in one meeting. Type 2 also includes those prospects who must either be sent information through the mail (or fax), and sold in a follow-up phone call, or those who cannot make a decision without "thinking it over." Instead of fruitlessly wasting your time trying to sell this kind of caller over the phone, you will want to "qualify" this prospect either to arrange an appointment for a sales presentation or to set up a follow-up phone call, to close the sale later.

The third type of prospect includes those who call for information but after you qualify them you decide you should go ahead and attempt to close the sale on the first call.

Since two out of three prospects may in fact be sold during the first call, you may want to look over the Telephone Sales Test below to see how many (if any) of your products or services can in fact be sold over the phone.

The Telephone Sales Test

1. Will customers be able to make up their minds about buying from information included in your advertising alone? Or can you explain the major features of your product or service—and close the sale—in only three to five minutes on the telephone?
2. Does only one person usually make the decision to buy?
3. Can payment or credit arrangements be immediately taken care of on the phone?
4. Is there any logical reason why customers could not purchase your products or services over the telephone?

If your products or services do not meet the Telephone Sales Test, you want to focus on turning telephone inquiries into qualified prospects, to be sold later in face-to-face presentations by appointment. If, on the other hand, you answered yes to the first three questions and no to the fourth, you obviously need to be sure you and your sales staff are fully prepared to be one-call closers on the telephone.

Regardless of their size, most successful businesses designate at least two persons (so someone is always there during breaks and lunch time) to handle telephone orders and answer callers' inquiries about the products or services they sell. No matter which employees are selected, they should not only be thoroughly familiar with the products and services your firm offers, but good business sense tells us:

Only those with the best phone skills should be entrusted with handling telephone orders and inquiries. Their success on the phone directly affects the gross income and profits of the entire enterprise.

Your inside sales staff or telemarketing operators should have mastered all the skills we've discussed so far, as well as the Top Ten Priorities covered in Chapter 2. Of course the first thing anyone answering calls for your sales staff will want to do is classify the prospect.

Determine if caller is ready to buy now.

The simplest way to save time and find out what kind of prospect you have on the line is by using an introduction with a "trial close." Remember to use a friendly, cheerful Telestyle as you . . .

Help the caller do business with your firm.

If you've been told the name of the caller . . .

Operator: "Good morning, Mr. Thompson, this is Jean Crane in Telemarketing. Which of our products (or services) may I help you order, today?"

If you don't know the name . . .

Sales: Sales Department. This is Jean Crane. Who's calling, please?"

Caller: "This is Jim Thompson. I'd like to talk with someone about your Widgets."

Sales: Well, thank you for calling me, Mr. Thompson. How many did you wish to order?"

This is the fastest way I know of for determining instantly if you have a Type 1 prospect or not. If they aren't ready to buy, they'll tell you: "Oh no, I just wanted to get some information." Later, we'll discuss how to "qualify" this type of caller to determine whether they are Type 2 or Type 3 prospects. If the caller indicates that he or she is ready to buy now (Type 1), then you are well on your way to providing fast, efficient service.

Increase Profits from Telephone Orders with Enthusiasm

Those who phone in their orders are obviously the easiest sales of all. They've already demonstrated their willingness to buy from your firm by calling in orders on their own initiative.

Add-ons means bigger profits.

If you have products or services that fit the Telephone Sales Test, provide your sales team with add-ons or "special offers" they can present to the caller. List three to five choices of products or services on 3 x 5 index cards that your sales people can keep by their phones as reminders: Accessories, matching pieces, service contracts, package deals, special offers, upgrading to deluxe models, discounts for larger orders, etc. Offer them special commissions on these add-on sales, and that will not only increase sales and profits for you, but may help your top people earn the kind of money it takes to keep them from going to work for your competitors.

Remember . . .

The "cost of sale" involved in attracting a prospective customer to phone in his order is the same, whatever the size of the order. The more you increase the total amount of the order, the more profitable the sale.

The extra gross profit that accrues to a larger order should allow you more than enough to offer incentives and/or discounts—to stimulate even more sales in the future.

First write up the order correctly. Then tactfully work to increase its profitability with add-ons, turning on the enthusiasm as you describe them. Remember the power of enthusiasm? Well . . .

Selling is by far the best way to use it for profit.

In Chapter 3 we discussed how you can become a want creator by raising the volume and speed of your voice to sound enthusiastic on the telephone. This technique is particularly important for increasing telephone orders, because it also speeds up the pace of the entire conversation. Remember . . .

Normally you will have only three to five minutes to present add-ons and write up the order.

The faster the pace of the conversation, the more it pays to be organized. First, confirm correct names, addresses, and phone numbers along with inventory codes, product descriptions, and all the shipping and credit information you will need to process the order correctly. This is also a good time to ask the caller how he or she was referred to your firm, so you can track results from advertising, promotions, and lead referral programs, etc. Write up the caller's initial order, but leave the total open. Double-check to be sure all codes or numbers for accounts, Purchase Orders or credit cards are written down accurately. Then enthusiastically present whatever add-ons or specials you feel the caller should know about. In fact . . .

Anyone handling telephone orders should make at least two attempts to increase each order.

One attempt is not enough, because the caller might not even hear the first offer. I believe in persistence, but there's a limit. Three attempts can still be made—sometimes—without offending the customer. But four or more attempts to increase an order will sound obnoxious and turn customers off. Present these offers as opportunities with a friendly, cheerful, enthusiastic Telestyle, and use a choice of two and other forced-response questions to make it easy for callers to say yes.

> Sales: **"Did you want to order just one set, or would you rather order three more for gifts, and save twenty percent on the total order?"**
>
> **"Yes, Mr. Johnson, we'll be glad to ship that out to you today. We have a deluxe model with a leather carrying case for $135, or would you prefer the executive model with the leather case and remote control for only $199?"**
>
> **"Ok, Ms. King, we'll be glad to send you a half-dozen cases by common carrier. But if you order a dozen we'll throw in an extra case and counter display as well. Do you want to stick with a half-dozen, or would you prefer to take advantage of this special offer and get more for your money, too?"**

Notice how the most profitable of the add-ons is always presented as the second of a choice of two? Remember, all you have to do is slightly raise the volume and speed of your voice to sound enthusiastic on the telephone. The more excited you sound, the more excited callers will become, and the easier it will be to help them buy more. Don't ask callers if they want to buy. Use an "assumptive close" instead.

> **Sales: "Yes, Ms. Collins, we have those in stock now. Should we ship them to your home or business address?"**

An assumptive close simply means you assume the callers want to buy the add-ons you've presented (they'll tell you if they don't), as you phrase your closing questions to lead them beyond the buying decision to focus on how the purchase, delivery, or other minor details will be handled.

> **Sales: "Mr. Sparks, we can process your order this afternoon and deliver your new widget with the accessories we've discussed tomorrow morning if someone will be there. Or would the afternoon be more convenient for you?"**
>
> **"Do you already have an account with us, Mr. Colvert, or would you rather just send us a check?"**
>
> **"You can take care of the order and service agreement with VISA, Master Card, or American Express. Which do you prefer?"**
>
> **"If you can wait a few days for delivery by common carrier, we'll pay all shipping costs ourselves. But if you're in a hurry, we can have it there tomorrow by overnight Express Mail for a small extra charge. How soon do you need it?"**

Some sales require a more subtle "lead-in" to presenting add-ons.

> **Try to discover—by means of a carefully phrased question— which features and benefits the caller finds most appealing about the firm's products or services.**

This kind of lead-in question not only helps you pinpoint the customer's interests, so you know which of your add-ons to talk about, it also helps you control the conversation and lead the caller from one topic to another. Depending of course upon the products or services you sell, your lead-in question might sound something like . . .

> Sales: "Thank you very much for ordering our widgets, Mr. Johnson. Do you mind if I ask how you'll be using them?"
>
> "Would you like for us to include a gift card, or are you ordering these for yourself?"
>
> "We do appreciate your patronage, Ms. King. And in order to improve, we're asking customers to help us evaluate our services. Which features of our service appeal to you the most, Ms. King?"

Be a good listener, and you will immediately identify ways to increase the order, as the customer resells himself on your products and services, while describing the features he appreciates or the ways he anticipates using them.

Once you identify the opportunity, present the add-on or special that logically fits the customer's needs or desires, and finish your statement with a choice of two as an assumptive close.

> Sales: "They do make wonderful gifts, Mr. Johnson. Customers with at least four people on their gift lists can save 20 percent, or get a fifth one for themselves, free. Would you rather save 20 percent in cash, Mr. Johnson, or does five for the price of four sound better to you?"
>
> "Widgets are great for shipping delicate instruments, particularly when you use our silicon packaging kits with them to protect against humidity. If you like, I can include a couple of dozen kits with your order for only $175. Or if you want to save a lot of money on future shipments, a full case of forty-eight is on sale right now for just $299. Which sounds best to you?"

> **"We've always been proud of our efficiency, Ms. King, and our new Teleconnect Service is saving many of our customers a lot of time processing their receivables. Most feel they save more than enough man-hours to justify the $75 per month rental, but some are signing up for three years for only $50 per month. Do you want to try it for a few months at the regular rate, or would you rather save $25 per month with our three-year program?"**

By emphasizing the most profitable add-on to begin with (the second of a choice of two), you can drop to less expensive choices and still increase the profitability of the order. If on the other hand you start out selling your least expensive add-on, you will not have anything lower to drop to.

> **"Sure you can sign up for one year, Ms. King. At just $65 per month you will still save $120 over the year. Would you like me to include a subscription to our newsletter as well?"**

Good sales sense tells us . . .

It is far easier to close a sale by dropping to a lower cost option than by moving up to a more expensive alternative.

Pay attention to how the caller reacts to what you are saying. Remember you've already made a sale. If you notice any sign of irritation on the customer's part as you present add-ons, quit. Don't be pushy. By the same token, once the customer has indicated his or her willingness to buy your add-ons, stop selling and total up the order.

Don't oversell.

If you continue to talk up the features of a product or service after a caller has agreed to buy it, you may irritate him so much you will talk yourself out of the sale.

Once you've confirmed the total, with or without add-ons . . .

Thank the caller for the order and <u>ask for referrals.</u>

This may not be appropriate for all businesses (funeral homes come to mind as an exception), but if you've got salespeople out in the field prospecting for referrals, common sense says you shouldn't miss the opportunity to ask for referrals from your telephone orders.

> Sales: **"I do appreciate your placing your order with me, Mr. Thompson. Who else do you know who might be interested in our services, too?"**
>
> **"Thank you very much for calling us, Ms. King. Are there other store owners in the mall you might want to refer us to as well?"**
>
> **"I hope you have a real nice holiday, Mr. Johnson. Who else do you know with a big Christmas list?"**

If you have built a friendly rapport with the customer during the conversation, he or she may well be disposed to give you several leads. Write down names with contact data and as much information about each prospect as the caller is willing to volunteer. If the caller cannot give you any names now, plant the seeds for harvest later.

> **"Thanks for trying, Mr. Thompson. If you think of someone later, give me a call or make a note. I'll probably be calling you in a few weeks anyway, just to be sure you're happy with your new widgets. Thanks again, Mr. Thompson, and if you ever need our assistance in any way, feel free to call me anytime."**

If you have developed a friendly relationship with the customer and your products or services are as presented, you may find your customer has quite a list of prospects prepared for you when you call. Of course some customers never give referrals, but every once in a while, you run into one who keeps on providing you with new leads year after year.

The more customers you ask for referrals, the more leads you will get, and the better your chances of finding super customers, who are endless sources of leads for future business.

You can neither cultivate nor harvest until after you have planted the seeds, however, so *don't forget to ask for referrals!*

Asking for referrals can also be a great way to sell add-ons or introduce new products or services by what is called the indirect approach. Using the indirect approach in sales is like fishing with a baited hook. You dangle the bait in front of the prospect in hopes he or she will nibble.

> **Sales: "Thank you for the order, Mr. Johnson. I'm sure you know others in similar businesses. Do you know anyone who might be interested in the unveiling of our brand-new fully automated packaging system next month?"**

The indirect approach is not only fun, it is a very soft sell.

What appears on the surface to be a simple request for referrals can (with an enthusiastic description) be turned into a subtle but very powerful means of arousing the customer's interest in your new product or service—without seeming to use any sales pressures at all.

The customer may or may not give you the names of referrals. However, if you have aroused the customer's interest, he or she may say, "That sounds like something I'd like to see for myself." Go ahead and close the sale if it is an add-on, or arrange an appointment for a face-to-face presentation.

> **Sales: "If you like, I could have one of our sales engineers drop by your office next week to give you a preview presentation. Would Monday be convenient, or would Tuesday morning be better for you?"**

Whether or not you are able to sell more add-ons, arrange presentations, or obtain additional referrals . . .

Be sure to read important information back to the caller to ensure accuracy before hanging up the phone.

Before turning in the order, check it over to be sure the writing is legible, so others can read it. There should be a space on your company's sales-order form to write in your name, so other employees will know whom to contact if they have questions about processing the order properly.

If a caller is already prepared to buy, you want to process his or her order as quickly and professionally as you can. However, if a caller says he or she just wants information, you must be able to answer the caller's questions while asking a series of your own to "qualify" the prospect *before* determining whether he or she is a Type 2 or Type 3 prospect. Start out by assuming that all non-Type 1 prospects are Type 2, those who must be sold face to face, or in two or more meetings or telephone conversations.

Qualify Prospects to Improve Closing Percentages

Many products and services must be sold in "presentations," where the features and benefits are presented to prospects in an organized manner. The percentage of presentations that result in successfully closed sales are referred to by the pros as their closing percentages. The sales person's most lasting success comes from concentrating upon ways to raise his or her closing percentages. While many presentations could stand improvement . . .

The most common reason sales presentations are missed is because sales reps fail to make sure they are presenting qualified prospects to begin with.

The criteria for evaluating prospects will vary considerably among different sales organizations, of course, but we can safely define a "qualified prospect" as one who . . .

. . . Has an interest in, desire for, or perceived need for the kinds of products or services your firm sells.

. . . Is financially able to buy from you now.

. . . Has the authority to make the decision to buy from you now.

. . . Is not presently under contract for an extended period of time to continue paying for similar products or services purchased from a competitor.

No matter how good a presentation your salespeople have, they will be wasting their time if they present it to prospects who do not meet *all four* criteria shown above. How can anyone be expected to sell something to people who are either not interested, can't afford it, don't have the authority to make the decision to buy it, or already have a competitor's model, which they are still obligated to pay for over a lengthy period of time?

Qualifying prospects when they call is a very cost-efficient way to help your salespeople use their time more productively. Except for the occasional spy from a competitor, anyone who calls to inquire about your products or services should be regarded as a prospect. Be sure that whoever answers such inquiries is well prepared. He or she must not only know how to answer questions, but also how to ask a series of prepared questions, to see if the caller does in fact meet all four criteria for a qualified prospect—one who should see (or hear) your sales presentation. Plan questions that lead callers to give you the information you need quickly. The following sample dialogues should give you some ideas.

Caller: "Oh no, I just wanted some information about your products."

Employee: "Certainly, Mr. Johnson, I'll be glad to put some information about our Widgets in the mail for you. Should I send it to your home or office?"

Caller: "Yes, send it to me at the XYZ Company."

Employee: "Yes, sir, the XYZ Company. Can you give me the address, please? (Get suite number, Zip Code, etc. then continue on) May I also get your phone number, Mr. Johnson, so we can call to confirm that you received the information requested?"

Caller: "Sure, that's 555–1231."

Employee: "555–1231. And may I have your title with the firm, Mr. Johnson, so I can address this package properly?"

Caller: "Yes, I'm the controller for our company."

Employee: "XYZ Company sounds familiar, Mr. Johnson. Are you already a customer of ours?"

Caller: "No, I don't think so."

Employee: "Have you been in business long?"

Caller: "We've been in business for eight years, but we're a small company with only sixteen employees."

Employee: "How were you referred to us?"

Caller: "Well, to tell you the truth, I picked your name out of the Yellow Pages."

Employee: "I'm glad you called us, Mr. Johnson. Can you give me an idea of how you hoped to use our products (services), so I'll know what specific information to include in your packet?"

Caller: "Yes, we were wondering if your Widgets could help us save time assembling oil rig components for shipment overseas. Do you have anything relating to oilfield applications?"

Employee: "I'll be happy to enclose whatever I can find. Are you using any similar products (services) now?"

Caller: "Well, we did buy a couple of cases of Wadgets three or four years ago, but we haven't used them in years."

Employee: "I'm sure you'll like our Widgets a lot better. Should I send extra packets of information for others involved in the selection process?"

Caller: "Oh, it would be nice if you could send two more for our operations manager and production supervisor?"

Employee: "Certainly, Mr. Johnson. In fact I'll address each envelope personally if you give me their names?"

Caller: "OK, Bill Thomas is our production supervisor, and Charolotte Webb is operations manager. You can send both their packets to this same address."

Employee: "I'll be happy to take care of it for you, Mr. Johnson. However one of our sales reps, Jack Youngblood, knows all about the oil patch. According to his schedule, Jack will be working in your area tomorrow.

Do you still want me to mail this information, or would you rather have Jack bring it with him to your offices sometime tomorrow, so he can answer any questions you or your associates might have on the spot?"

Caller: "That's quick service. When could he stop by?"

Employee: "Well, I'm sure you'd want to include Ms. Webb and Mr. Thomas in the meeting. Could you all be free to meet with Jack tomorrow morning at, say, 9:30, or would right after lunch be better for you?"

One of the primary points to remember if you are handling inquiries from callers is. . . .

Write down contact information first.

Then if you are unexpectedly interrupted or disconnected you can call back to complete the conversation. If time doesn't permit you to qualify the prospect fully, you can still give the prospect's name and contact information to your sales rep.

Offering to send literature is an easy way of obtaining callers' business names, job titles (are they decision makers?), and addresses. Phone numbers are then obtained when you offer to confirm that literature is received. Notice how the employee in this example tactfully led into asking how long the caller's business has been operating? Questions like "How long have you been in business?" or "How many employees do you have?" help you determine if a prospect is in fact financially able to buy. If your customers are private consumers, you may need to ask about employment and home ownership, etc.

Sales: "We have a lot of customers from that part of town. What kind of work do you do out there, Mr. Thompson?"

"I've heard there are some nice neighborhoods in your area. Do you live in an apartment or did you buy a home out there, Ms. King?"

Offering to send additional packets of information is a great way to learn the names and titles of others who may be involved in buying decisions. As you can see, questions about how products will be used or what the caller already has are easy to insert into the conversation logically.

Determine the prospect's reasons for interest in your products or services.

Don't just qualify a prospect on what he or she needs. Hopes and desires could very well motivate him even more.

The more you can encourage a prospect to talk about what he wants, the easier it will be to make him want what you are selling.

The following sample questions should give you some ideas . . .

Sales: "Ideally how do you hope to use our products?"

"What are the most important features you're looking for?"

"How did you become interested in our services?"

"Is this for business or private use?"

"Who will be using it most?"

"How will a service (or product) like this benefit your business?"

"Do you remember what first caught your eye in our ad?"

Listen to the prospect's answers, and try to read between the lines. Is this prospect more interested in the lowest price or most technically advanced features? Is he stressing service or long-term warranties? If you have a hard time getting a prospect to open up, stimulate him to expand his answers with little prodding questions like "Oh?" or "Really?"

Remember . . .

The purpose of qualifying a prospect is to find out if he or she is in fact the kind of prospect you may reasonably expect to sell.

Make sure you ask questions, based upon the unique requirements of your particular business, that will tell you everything you need to know before arranging a formal presentation or demonstration.

The more you know about a prospect, the better you can focus your presentation upon his or her specific requirements.

Most callers will be very cooperative in answering your questions. They want you to understand their needs and interests, so that you can give them the kind of information they need and furnish reliable cost estimates.

After you have determined that the caller is a qualified Type 2 prospect . . .

Arrange a definite appointment for him to be presented either by phone, at his office, or in your firm's showroom as soon as possible.

A choice of two makes arranging such appointments a snap . . .

Sales: **"I'll put this information in the mail for you this afternoon, Mr. Thompson, and plan on giving you a follow-up call Thursday morning at 9:15—unless 11:45 would be better for you. Which looks best on your calendar?**

"I realize how difficult it is to evaluate something you've never seen, so why don't I bring one out for you and your office manager to look at tomorrow afternoon, Mr. Johnson. Or would Wednesday be better for the two of you?"

"Did you want to run by our showroom for a test drive this afternoon, Ms. King? Or would you rather stop off on the way in to work tomorrow morning?"

Occasionally you will have to qualify a prospect *after* arranging an appointment. After all, if someone calls your office to request that you send a sales representative out to see him, you will certainly not want to hesitate. The same for anyone who wants to arrange an appointment to visit your premises to learn about your products or services. First use a choice of two to arrange the appointment.

Caller: "I wonder if you could send someone over to see us who can explain the various kinds of packaging equipment your firm sells?"

Employee: "Why, certainly, Mr. Adams. Would three o'clock tomorrow afternoon be soon enough, or would ten o'clock tomorrow morning be better for you?"

Caller: "Ten A.M. is perfect for me if you can get someone out here that soon?"

Employee: "No problem, Mr. Adams. Would you give me the name and address of your firm, along with directions for finding it, and your phone number in case we have to reschedule, please?"

Once you have written down all necessary contact information, ask whatever questions you need to qualify the prospect properly.

Employee: "I'd like to ask you a couple of questions about your operations if you don't mind, Mr. Adams. That's so our rep can be better prepared for this meeting. What kinds of materials will you be packaging?"

Some callers will indicate they are in too big a hurry to answer a bunch of questions. Others will just want to know your prices or rates. If you are friendly, cheerful, and courteous, and ask logical questions in a tactful way, you will still be able to qualify most of these callers, too. Those who seem most reluctant to give you any information at all may be spying for your competition. If you become suspicious of a caller's motives, cannot get answers to your questions, don't have time to qualify a prospect, or for any reason you do not feel competent to help the caller properly, handle it this way.

Employee: "I'm sorry I don't have the expertise to give you the help you need, Mr. Johnson. But I can have someone

> **who is qualified call you back in a few minutes, if you'll give me your phone number, please?" (If the caller is a spy for a competitor, he will probably not want to leave a number.)**

If you are not supposed to quote rates or prices over the phone, you might say . . .

> **Sales: "I don't have that information in front of me now, but I can have someone with a price list call you back later this morning, or would after lunch be better for you?"**

> Or set up a face-to-face sales presentation.

> **"In order to keep our fees as low as possible, we compute our rates according to the unique complexities of each assignment. I'll be happy to send someone out to your office who can give you a free estimate down to the penny. Will you be in tomorrow, or would Thursday be more convenient for you?"**

Rather than chance blowing a possible sale by irritating an impatient caller or giving out the wrong information, take a message and have one of your sales reps call back to qualify the prospect himself. It doesn't matter who asks the questions as long as you make sure to qualify prospects before beginning a sales presentation.

Turn Inquiries into Sales on the First Calls

If after qualifying the prospect you believe you have a Type 3 prospect—one you might be able to persuade to buy during the first call—use the information he or she has volunteered to present your product or service in ways that are most appealing to the prospect, and offer a reason to buy now. Instead of saying "you" all the time, present your products in the third person by drawing mental pictures the prospect wants to be in.

Sales: "Most people really appreciate the convenience of a remote control, so they can make adjustments on a hot day without having to put down their cool drinks and go out in the heat. Can you see why this is one of our most popular features with people like us who live in the sunbelt, Mr. Thompson?"

If a salesperson keeps saying "*you* can do this, *you* ought to have such and such, *you* should buy, *you* can save, *you* can use," etc., the prospect will feel high-pressured and throw up objections and other defenses to resist this pressure. Talking in the third person about how other people, customers, businesses, families, etc. save money using your products and the benefits they enjoy places no pressure upon the prospect whatsoever. In fact, this kind of reverse psychology actually makes the prospect want to be one of those people saving all that money and reaping all those benefits you're talking about. See what I mean by "drawing mental pictures the prospect wants to be in"?

Turn on the enthusiasm when drawing those mental pictures, and you really will become a powerful want creator.

Get the word "you" out of your sales vocabulary, unless of course you are asking "commitment questions." A sales pro asks a commitment question so the prospect hears himself committing to seeing the benefits, wanting the product or service, or believing he or she can afford it. Those commitments not only lead the prospect to buy, they also give a salesperson something to fall back on if the prospect starts to waiver in the late stages of a presentation.

Phrase your questions in such a way as to get the prospect in the habit of answering yes, and he or she will almost naturally continue to answer yes when you ask to write up the order.

Seller: "Can you see why many people are ordering now to save as much as 25 percent?"

"Most of our customers really appreciate our same-day delivery plan, Mr. Johnson. Will someone be there this afternoon, or should we plan on delivering your new machine tonight after you get home from work?"

Don 't argue if the caller objects at first. Stay friendly and use Reverses instead.

Prospect: "I need to think about it."

Seller: "I don't blame you for giving this kind of investment a lot of thought. In fact we spent a lot of time and money developing a product our customers will be proud to own for years to come. If we shipped this model out to you today and everything I've said were guaranteed in writing with a ten-year warranty, would you feel like you'd made a wise investment, Mr. Thompson?"

Prospect: "Man, that's a lot of money."

Seller: "Yes, it's a major investment, but can you see why most of our customers feel it is a small price to pay when one considers that all mechanical worries are virtually eliminated for the next ten years?"

Prospect: "I don't know if I can afford it."

Seller: "I realize such a program could be difficult for some people to afford if they had to take care of it all at once, but can you see how our budget plan makes it easy for anyone who really wants it to have it?"

Prospect: "Doesn't XYZ Company make these, too?"

Seller: "They make some fine products, but ours work better and last longer, and if you take advantage of this special offer, the overall costs run almost half what they charge. Doesn't this seem like a wiser investment to you?"

Prospect: "Three years is a long time to be obligated."

Seller: "Yes, sir, and the beautiful part is that it's all guaranteed in writing. Do you feel we've gone far enough to ensure our customer's satisfaction?"

Prospect: "I just don't know."

Seller (Falling back on commitments): "Well, I know you want to make the right choice, so let's look at what we've already agreed upon. You did say you appreciated the benefits, thought it was affordable, would satisfy your needs completely, and that you really want it. Can you think of any logical reason why you shouldn't go ahead

and start the program now? Or are you ready to start saving money right away?"

Plan a brief, truthful sales presentation of only two or three sentences (loaded with descriptions of benefits), combined with commitment questions that you can enthusiastically deliver in about three minutes on the phone. Prepare honest answers in advance, using the Teletactics we've discussed for the most common questions or objections you are likely to hear in your business. Use Forced Response questions to make your assumptive close sound like the most logical reason to buy now, and write up the order as discussed for Type 1 prospects. Present add-ons as explained earlier and don't forget to ask for referrals. You will turn a lot of inquiries into very profitable sales on the first calls.

Convert Complaints into Endorsements

Many businesses never see the value of a complaint call. Value? Read on. I certainly hope most of your customers or clients are satisfied with your products or services, so much so that they never give it a second thought. The complainer, on the other hand, is very likely to vent his frustrations loudly to everyone he knows.

When a dissatisfied customer becomes frustrated enough to call and complain, you have a unique opportunity to turn that complaint into public praise.

If you are willing to invest in your public reputation and use the right Teletactics, you might even end up with an endorsement letter. Complaints offer a unique opportunity for a company to build a reputation for superior quality service.

Begin by *agreeing* with the customer's right to be upset, *apologize* for causing it, and *thank* the caller for bringing the problem to your attention so you can correct it. Then establish control with a question designed to *get the caller to describe the problem fully*.

Employee: "I don't blame you for being so upset, Ms. King, and we are very sorry you feel one of our products caused it. I do appreciate your calling to give us the opportunity to demonstrate what we mean by quality service. Will you tell me exactly what happened, please?"

Maybe your product or service is not at fault, but if you apologize for being part of the problem, the caller will feel you are properly sympathetic to his or her needs.

Admit concern—not liability.

Every company should be concerned with customer satisfaction, but don't make any admissions your legal department might chastise you for later.

The key to good service is *listening*.

Customer Service is a tough job that requires the ability to listen attentively with a thick skin.

Prompt an irate caller as often as necessary to allow him to vent all of his frustrations on you (that is what you get paid for) as he tells the whole story.

Often as not customers get frustrated with new products they are not familiar with, and as frustrations mount, they fail to think rationally enough to follow basic instructions in the operating manual. Even if they are at fault, you must let them pour out their feelings. Only when they have gotten the frustration out of their system will they be able to think or communicate rationally. Then they may be encouraged to go back and resolve the problem themselves by following instructions.

Don't offer evaluations or make suggestions until you know all the facts—and until the irate customer has calmed down enough to understand what you are saying.

If you maintain a friendly, helpful attitude, encouraging the client to talk out his troubles, even the most abusive complainers will calm down quickly.

Write down the details of the caller's complaint for your records and read it back to him to be sure you understand completely all aspects of the problem.

Then ask . . .

Employee: "Does this described the problem accurately, or is there anything else you'd like to add?"

Hearing you read his complaint back over the phone and knowing you understand his problem will reassure him that he has gotten his message across. If he has anything else to add, write that down, too. Then *find out what the customer wants*.

Employee: "How may we correct the problem to your satisfaction?"

"We are very sorry for any inconvenience you've experienced with one of our products, and appreciate the opportunity to save a good customer. Ideally how would you like to see us handle it for you, Ms. King?"

"What would you like for us to do to make it right?"

"At this point, what can we do to make you a satisfied customer?"

If the customer's request is not totally unreasonable, and you have the authority to approve it, go ahead and do it quickly.

If you don't have the authority to approve the customer's request, offer to present it to your manager and call back within a couple of hours with a solution or status report. Stay in touch with the customer on a regular basis until the problem is resolved to the customer's satisfaction.

Once the problem is resolved, <u>ask for an endorsement.</u>

Why not? If you have been friendly, courteous, and helpful in solving problems for a customer, that customer will probably appreciate the personal attention he or she has received from you.

> **Employee: "Well, I'm sorry we met under such distressing circumstances, Ms. King, but I am glad we got everything taken care of for you. I wonder if you'd mind dropping us a brief note, giving your honest evaluation of our customer service? It would mean a lot to me personally, if it wouldn't be too much of an inconvenience?"**

If you have provided quality service with a friendly, cheerful Telestyle, chances are the customer will write a very complimentary letter. Such endorsements will not only help avoid problems later (it's difficult to justify a lawsuit after writing letters of praise), but will look very impressive in your employment record—particularly during performance and salary reviews. Companies may even request their customers' permission (usually granted) to show these letters to potential customers.

If a customer is seeking unreasonable damages or other forms of compensation, and you cannot tactfully reduce his demands to something within your authority, you would be wise to . . .

Refer the problem to your legal department.

However, if you listen courteously, maintaining a helpful and patient attitude, while the customer vents his frustrations, you can avoid most unpleasantness. Most complainers will appreciate your friendly sincerity and (often embarrassed over their behavior) will try to work with you. If you handle complaint calls with a combination of Teletactics and an all-out commitment to quality service, formerly irate customers will be telling friends and business associates—probably the same ones they were complaining to earlier—what a fine organization yours is. Chances are they will be more than willing to write you a complimentary letter, too. Converting complaints into endorsements is by far the best way to influence such calls for profit.

Screen Calls for Greater Productivity

Many executives ask their secretaries and assistants to screen their calls in order to manage their time more productively. There is a definite advantage to knowing the caller's identity, company, and purpose of the call before beginning a conversation. The callee can then be sure to have the proper file or data in front of him and thus be prepared for the conversation before picking up the phone.

> **Secretary: "Mr. Johnson's office. This is Mary Taylor. Who's calling please?"**
>
> Caller: "This is Robert Walker, is he in?"
>
> **Secretary: "I'll be happy to check for you, Mr. Walker. Will he know what company you're with?"**
>
> Caller: "I'm with J & B International. Is he available now?"
>
> **Secretary: "Let me see for you, Mr. Walker. May I tell him what the call is about?"**

Work with your assistant to coordinate your phone tactics in advance. You may want to prepare a PC list (priority callers) with the names of people whose calls should always be put through without screenings, plus an S list of people, or descriptions of the kinds of calls you do not normally wish to deal with. If you use such lists, review them with your assistant every four to six weeks to keep them up to date. Remember to inform your secretary or assistant when you are expecting exceptions—that is, priority calls from people whose names are not on your PC list. It is also a good idea to keep your assistant abreast of your normal routine for returning calls, too, so he or she can tell callers when they may expect to hear back from you.

Secretaries and assistants with years of experience are often given the authority to answer questions and help many callers themselves, when requests do not require the executive's personal attention. Guidelines should be provided by the executive in advance, so limits of authority are clear.

> **Secretary: "He's involved in an important project right now, Mr. Johnson, but I'll be glad to help you for him—if you'll tell me the purpose of your call, please?"**

Most secretaries and assistants rely upon three basic questions to screen the majority of calls: "Who's calling, please?", "What company are you with?", and "May I tell him [her] the nature of your call, please?" If the caller's name or company is on your boss's PC list, you can put the call through without asking the purpose of the call. If you do not recognize either, then learning the nature of the call should help you decide the best way to process the call from there.

> **"I'll be glad to see if she's free, Mr. Youngblood. May I prepare her for the nature of your call?"**

Most callers will be cooperative because they want you to save their time, too. A few may resent questioning by those they view as "underlings," but the majority of those who are not already on the boss's PC list and do not want to volunteer information are probably either selling something, seeking employment, or may (justifiably) fear that if they tell you what the call is about they won't be put through. An easy way to screen such calls is by asking . . .

> **"Does he know you, Mr. Jackson?"**

or

> **"Will she know what your call is about?"**

Even the most polished salespeople stumble over these questions because they will not want to lie, and end up angering the executive they are trying to reach. But one cannot overlook the possibility of a legitimate need for confidentiality either. Teletactics like the Politician's Ploy, Truitt's Law, and the Reverse will help you handle temperamental callers and delicate situations tactfully:

> **"I can certainly appreciate your need for confidentiality, Mr. Johnson, but Ms. Plummer has been very busy lately. I cannot give your call a priority rating without knowing a little more about it. Is there anything you can tell me so I can help you?"**

The most difficult calls to screen will probably be from salespeople. If you suspect the caller is trying to sell something and your boss wants you to screen sales calls . . .

"May I tell her what kinds of products or services you wish to discuss?"

Some executives will want you to request that salespeople present proposals in writing, first.

"In order to be fair to all vendors, Mr. Johnson requests that you mail whatever information you think he should see, along with a current price list—first. If he wants to know more, he will contact you himself. Would you like our mailing address, Mr. Thompson?"

This same technique is also recommended when executives want calls from charities and fund-raisers screened, too. If the caller tells you he or she is seeking employment . . .

"Mr. Johnson usually asks for a résumé first. If he is interested, he'll call back. If not, he will pass it on to our personnel department. If they have something for you, they will get right back to you. Otherwise you might not hear from us at all. Does that sound fair enough to you?"

Remember: Just because you've been asked to screen calls does not mean you should forget any of the Top Ten Priorities. Your first responsibility is still to make a good impression. Use a friendly, courteous Telestyle as you handle your duties, and keep the mood of the conversation as cheerful as possible. Even those you have to screen will appreciate the nice way you did it. If you are ever in doubt as to the best way to handle a call . . .

Ask the boss or take a message.

If your boss cannot be disturbed, get as much information as you can on a message memo and let the boss evaluate the call himself, later on. You would certainly not want to risk insulting or irritating an important caller, because you failed to understand the significance of the call.

Screen Responses to Employment Ads

Screening responses to Help Wanted ads will save a lot of time for your Personnel Department and help you avoid unnecessary interviews. But the ad itself can be written so as to telegraph certain information automatically.

Use a fake name for the person to contact in your employment ad. Then whoever answers the phone will know what the call is about as soon as the caller asks for the false name. If you are running several different ads, different names will allow you to determine immediately which ad the caller is responding to. This can also help you keep certain information confidential before the interview if necessary. Plan questions that will help you quickly determine if you have a "value applicant" or not.

Prepare a series of questions to use when the applicant calls. If you've run an attractive ad in the Sunday classifieds, your phones will literally be ringing off the hook on Monday morning, especially if you are advertising for trainees. Most callers will have questions of their own about the job, salary, and company itself. If you don't seize immediate control of the call with questions, you will find that the callers are doing the controlling. Moreover if you are getting a large number of calls, you won't have time to answer a lot of questions. That could defeat the purpose of running an attractive ad in the first place, by tying up your phone lines.

Employee: "Executive Offices, may I help you?"

Caller: "Yes, may I speak to Mr. Fortson, please?"

Employee: "He's not available right now. Are you calling about the ad in the paper?"

Caller: "Yes I am."

Employee: "Fine, I need to ask you some preliminary questions. What is your name, please?"

Caller: "Joe Baker."

Employee: "OK Mr. Baker, can you tell me the extent of your formal education, please?"

Caller: "I graduated from college with a degree in Business Administration."

Employee: "And are you presently employed?"

Caller: "Oh yes. I've been with the same employer for the past four years."

Employee: "What kind of work do you do now, Mr. Baker?"

Caller: "I sell hot tubs for a local department store."

Employee: "OK, Mr. Baker, let me ask you this—if you were to find suitable employment with us, how soon would you be available to start?"

Notice how easily and efficiently "ad calls" are handled when you control conversations with a prepared list of screening questions? Of course you will want to . . .

Use questions about the specific qualifications you are looking for in a value applicant.

You will not be able (or even want) to interview everyone who calls. In fact, the main reasons for screening such calls is to ensure that only the very best qualified candidates are interviewed for the position you wish to fill. If callers do not meet your basic criteria, you may end the conversation here . . .

Employee: "We can only interview those applicants who already have the specific experience we advertised for, Mr. Baker, but we do appreciate your taking the time to call."

Be sure to avoid asking any discriminatory questions about the caller's age (unless you suspect the caller is a minor) sex, race, religion, or national origin.

As stated earlier, a fake name in an employment ad also helps you avoid lengthy discussions or divulging too much information on the phone.

Employee: "I am sorry, but Mr. Fortson has not authorized me to give out any details over the phone. All of your questions will be answered in the interview, however, if you can come in tomorrow afternoon at 2 P.M. Or would three o'clock be better for you?"

Here again, a choice of two is the quickest way to confirm an appointment without haggling back and forth to determine the best times for everyone. Use a legal pad or prepare a form to help you keep track of data on callers, their answers to your questions, and appointment schedules. A log will also help you evaluate responses to your ads and help determine which produced the best results. If you record each applicant's phone number, you will be able to change schedules or cancel later interviews after you have hired someone.

Master Defensive Strategies to Prepare Your Offense

The examples in this chapter should give you more ideas for ways to influence incoming calls for greater profit and productivity. Be as creative as you like with your ideas. The ability to take charge of incoming calls quickly and influence the outcome with Telestyle and Teletactics will help you deal productively with a variety of calls from employees, fellow workers, vendors, customers, and even your employer.

Group role-play sessions can be very effective for teaching the techniques described in this chapter to telemarketing organizations, sales professionals, customer-service and personnel departments, secretaries, and executive assistants as well. The more you practice the skills and tactics we've discussed with your incoming calls, the more productive and profitable they will be.

Chapters 2 through 4 have described Phone Tactics for incoming calls, which are basically defensive by nature, because someone else has already taken the initiative when he or she placed the call in the first place. In the next four chapters, we'll be on the offensive, placing outbound calls ourselves. Your knowledge of the defensive strategies discussed here will better prepare you to overcome them if necessary when you are the caller on other end of the line.

5

PLAN A
TELESEARCH FOR
ANYTHING YOU WANT

O ver the years we seem to have conditioned ourselves to some outmoded notions concerning outbound telephone calls to strangers. With the exception of a few sales pioneers, most people tend to act as if they should never call someone they don't know without an introduction by a mutual acquaintance, or writing a query letter beforehand. Even networkers feel they have to resort to name-dropping when telephoning people they don't know: "So-and-so suggested I call."

People who need these getting-up-the-nerve preliminaries lack confidence in their ability to communicate effectively with strangers by phone. Such roundabout introductions cause delays and waste time and money. They have been particularly costly for those who fail to pursue their dreams because they "don't have the right contacts." So-and-so is a crutch you will never need if you combine the skills we've already discussed with the TELESEARCH strategies and other phone tactics described in this book.

Telesearch eliminates any need for third party introductions, advance mailings, query letters, and other needless preliminaries when cold calling people you don't know.

A Telesearch is like a straight line. It is the shortest distance between you and the person you ultimately need to communicate with to get the results you want. I first used the term "Telesearch" to describe a very fast method of using the phone to find employment, by talking with department heads directly. A personnel agency in Boston uses the same term to describe the method their consultants use to recruit talent. The fact is . . .

You can use the telephone to search for anything. All you need is an easy-to-follow plan of action and the phone skills to make it work.

A Telesearch is a planned, professional approach that will help you use the skills and tactics described in this book to save time and money. Below is just a partial listing of what you can find by using a Telesearch Plan:

Lowest rates and prices	Missing persons
Data on new technology	Video and film producers
Rare collectibles	Professional advice
Government loans	Agents and talent
Sales prospects	Special schools
New clients	Research information
Names for networking	Opinion surveys
Executive talent	Doctors and dentists
Experienced workers	New homes for pets
Donors and contributors	Publicity
Political support	Guest speakers
New investors	New members
Travel data and discounts	A dinner date
Attorneys, CPAs	Product information
The ideal new home	"Inside information"
Office facilities	Employment opportunities
Data for school work	Relocation assistance

Market research data	Publishers
New markets	Markets for creative work
All kinds of referrals	Technical assistance
All kinds of information	Casting offices
Volunteers for a cause	Colleges and scholarships
Business opportunities	Interviews with celebrities
Help for charities	Community services
Venture capitalists	Veterinarians
Domestic help	Discounts on anything
Repair people	TV and radio appearances
Business locations	Seminar participants
Consultants and agents	All kinds of customers
Investment information	Gigs for performers

What do you want to do? Whatever it is, a Telesearch can immediately put you in direct contact with the person or people who can help you accomplish it. It can help you gather information or distribute it, save money or earn it, arrange appointments to see virtually anyone, and influence a myriad of decisions that may affect your income, career, home life, job performance, business success, etc.

Although we cannot fully describe every application, the primary objectives of all Telesearch calls fall into three broad groups:

1. Calls seeking information.
2. Calls to arrange appointments.
3. Calls to influence decisions.

This chapter will help you develop a basic Telesearch Plan for anything, but focus specifically on calls for information, i.e.—obtaining advice, product info, research data, locating decision makers, prospecting and obtaining names and referrals, etc. Chapters 6 and 7 will help you follow your Telesearch Plan with the phone skills you to need get through to decision makers and arrange appointments. Chapter 8 will focus on getting faster results with advanced phone tactics for solving problems and influencing important decisions instantly.

There are seven basic steps in any Telesearch Plan, beginning with . . .

Step 1: Develop a Strategy to Reach Your Specific Goals

Whatever you want to accomplish, break it down into the individual steps you will have to take to reach your ultimate goal. If you're seeking employment, where are you worth the most? The magic of a Telesearch approach for job seekers is that they are not limited by what's advertised, or the type of openings that search firms and personnel agencies are trying to fill.

Telesearch helps you find the type of career opportunity you really want, instead of trying to fit into whatever is available.

If you're planning a career move, what specific position do you *really* want? What would be almost as good for a second choice? Third choice? Which companies normally employ people in those positions? Who would be your boss if you got the job you really wanted? What would his or her job title most likely be? How many interviews will you need to guarantee a selection of attractive job offers?

If you're planning a Telesearch for more sales, who are the best prospects to call? Where do you find them? How many presentations do you have to give to sell what you want? How many prospects do you need to qualify in order to line up that number of presentations? How many calls do you need to initiate daily to find that number of prospects? What are your best sources of leads?

If you want to find the lowest rates, fares, or prices, what kinds of companies or businesses will you need to call? Who within those organizations will have the power to give you a discount? What product information, model numbers, lists of options or accessories do you want near you by the phone when you call? How many calls will you have to complete to be sure you obtain the best deal?

If you need information, what kinds of people should have it? Where do they work? Job titles? Who is the best person to contact? What questions will you ask? How many should you call to be certain of finding the right answers?

Whatever your ultimate goals, look at where you are now and where you wish to end up. Write out a list of the steps you will most likely have to take to get from here to there. As you develop your overall strategy, how many steps along the way include people contact? Look at the task or goal you've set for yourself, and if it includes contacting people for any reason, a Telesearch can help you save time and expense contacting those people directly by phone.

Define the purpose of each call as it relates to reaching your ultimate goals.

Will you be seeking information, an appointment, a decision, or any combination of the three? These then are the specific goals of each Telesearch call.

Step 2: Profile Your Priority Contact (Person to Call)

Once you know what you want, identify the people who either have it or can help you get it. Answer the following questions as objectively as you can:

1. What types of people will most likely be my Priority Contacts, who have the resources and/or authority to help me now?
2. Which of my personal or professional acquaintances are such people, or would know these Priority Contacts?
3. Which schools, churches, clubs, professional or trade associations would such people belong to?
4. What kinds of businesses or organizations employ such people?
5. In which departments would they be employed?
6. What are their job titles most likely to be?

Whom do you need to call? An employer, business owner, head of a household, executive assistant, corporate officer, service manager, repairman, domestic servant, technician, buyer, store manager, etc.? If, for instance, you're looking for the best price on a big-ticket item like a large-screen TV, automobile, tractor, major appliance, or personal computer, you will obviously want to talk to dealers. *If you are buying in quantity*, contact wholesalers, distributors, manufacturer's reps or the manufacturer's vice president of sales (or marketing). If it is a small firm, you will probably want to talk with the owner or president.

Regardless of the size of the firm, when you are seeking a discount, always bypass individual salespeople by contacting the person in charge of the sales force directly.

Some kind of commission incentive is virtually always used to stimulate sales of big-ticket items. If you bypass the salespeople and talk to the man on top—store manager, sales manager, regional, district or national sales manager, VP sales and marketing, owner or president, depending of course upon the size of the firm and purchase involved—you will automatically eliminate his or her need to pay commissions on your sales to those further down the chain of command. Therein lies the beginning of a discount.

If you're involved in any kind of executive search or recruiting assignment, profile the person who satisfies the Big Three requirements. The ideal candidate is one who . . .

1. Can handle the job successfully
2. Is the type of individual who will succeed in your organization
3. Will want the job opportunity you have to offer

The applicant who fits all three is your Priority Contact. Is there a second- or third-choice candidate who might also fit the Big Three? What kinds of job titles are usually given (by what kinds of companies) to those who meet your profile? These are the Priority Contacts you will want to talk with directly.

If you are in sales, your priority contact will be the person with the authority to buy now.

This may not always be the buyer or purchasing agent however. In fact some firms use buyers and purchasing agents to screen calls from unknown sales reps for their superiors.

The real decision maker is usually the manager, department head, officer, or executive who tells the company's buyers and purchasing agents what to buy for his or her organization.

If you're seeking employment, your Priority Contact is the person who would be your boss if you got the job you wanted, not the Personnel Department (unless you want a job in personnel).

Personnel screens—management hires!

You don't want to be screened, you want to be hired. If you can induce the boss to want you in his or her organization, he or she will help you get through the Personnel Department's screening procedures: "Jim, this is Jack Thompson in Engineering. I've found a young engineer I want to hire in my group. Would you meet with her this afternoon to explain our benefit programs and check her references for me, please? I'd like to get her on board as soon as possible." See the difference the right Priority Contact can make?

Who has the information you need or the power to make the decisions you wish to influence? This is your Priority Contact, the person you need to call to get the information or results you want. Write out a brief profile of your Priority Contact, including type of business or other affiliation, job title, relationship, level of competence or authority, etc., and read it back to yourself. Does this brief profile describe the kind of person(s) you need to talk with so anyone would be able to understand it? Is there a second or third choice of Priority Contact who might be helpful, too? Profile those other secondary contacts as well. Now that you have a clear description of the types of people you want to contact, the next step is to come up with their actual names.

Step 3: Develop Your Resources

No matter what you're looking for—if it does exist—there are people, businesses, organizations, institutions, government agencies, and other resources available to help you find it.

One of the best resources available to anyone seeking product information, discounts, lower prices, rates, or competitive bids is of course the Yellow Pages. Names of key people do not normally appear in Yellow Page listings, but it is a quick reference for finding the names and phone numbers of all local businesses and organizations involved in a particular field (which you may then cross-reference with other sources). Yellow Page listings are organized according to products or services, presented alphabetically, but it is sometimes necessary to try several forms of generic names before you locate what you're looking for ("car repair" under "Automobile Servicing and Repair," for example).

You can obtain the actual names and titles of the Priority Contacts you need by cross-referencing with other sources (we'll discuss this below). Or use a quick preliminary phone call (see Chapter 1) or the Letter Technique:

> Reception: "XYZ Company, may I help you?"
>
> **Caller: "Yes, I need to address a note to your vice president of sales. Can you give me his or her name and the correct spelling, please?"**
>
> Reception: "Certainly. Mr. J. W. Thompson is our vice president of sales. That's spelled T-h-o-m-p-s-o-n."
>
> **Caller: "I'd like to personalize this message. Can you give me his first name or what his friends call him?"**
>
> Reception: "I don't really know his first name, but all his friends call him Bill."

Sometimes you can get the names of Priority Contacts from friends, relatives, and other personal acquaintances who are knowledgeable in the field of your inquiry.

> **Caller: "Hi, Janice, I need your help. Tesia is writing a report on transatlantic shipping for school. Who at your shipping company could she interview for her project?"**

If yours is a major project, a trip to the public library in the nearest city should help you find a variety of directories in the library's Business Reference Section. Directories are excellent sources for obtaining the names of specific people in business, government, industry, health care, the professions, education, politics, the arts, and any other field. Numerous city, county, state, national, and international directories have been published for virtually every kind of business, occupation, product, service, or other endeavor. *Standard & Poors Register Of Corporations, Directors & Executives* may well be the best of the national directories of major corporations, but there are thousands of local directories that will give you many more names of those involved in small business, government, and various professional and technical fields. Ask your librarian for assistance.

Regardless of the field you are researching, you want directories listing the key people in that particular field.

Whatever you want, there is a directory or data base available which can provide the names of those you need to call to get it. CompuServe and other computer services and software packages allow you to tap into all kinds of networks and directories via your personal computer's telephone modem. Your local Chamber of Commerce may publish directories of local firms. Your own corporate library may have numerous trade directories on hand now. Many sales departments have directories of businesses they sell to, while most purchasing departments keep directories of various types of suppliers, too. Some private organizations and trade associations still furnish membership lists free, although most will charge for them if they believe you will use them in sales. If, however, you need only two or three names, you can usually get those over the phone free.

> Recept: "West Houston Hackers Club. This is Julie. May I help you?"
>
> **Caller: "I hope so. I'm thinking of purchasing a telephone modem for my personal computer, and wondered if I might talk to two or three of your members to get some ideas. Who in your group would you recommend I contact first, Julie?"**

Be as resourceful as you can when looking for names. If you're in sales, files on your current and former customers should be helpful for prospecting. Employers wishing to recruit experienced workers and executives will find a wealth of names on employment

FIGURE 7: **TELESEARCH LIST**

DATE: _____   PAGE _____ OF _____

PURPOSE: _____   CALLER: _____

1. PH # _____   CO: _____   FOLLOW-UP: _____
   NAME: _____   TITLE: _____   SOURCE: _____
   RESULTS: _____

2. PH # _____   CO: _____   FOLLOW-UP: _____
   NAME: _____   TITLE: _____   SOURCE: _____
   RESULTS: _____

3. PH # _____   CO: _____   FOLLOW-UP: _____
   NAME: _____   TITLE: _____   SOURCE: _____
   RESULTS: _____

4. PH # _____   CO: _____   FOLLOW-UP: _____
   NAME: _____   TITLE: _____   SOURCE: _____
   RESULTS: _____

5. PH # _____   CO: _____   FOLLOW-UP: _____
   NAME: _____   TITLE: _____   SOURCE: _____
   RESULTS: _____

6. PH # _____   CO: _____   FOLLOW-UP: _____
   NAME: _____   TITLE: _____   SOURCE: _____
   RESULTS: _____

7. PH # _____   CO: _____   FOLLOW-UP: _____
   NAME: _____   TITLE: _____   SOURCE: _____
   RESULTS: _____

8. PH # _____   CO: _____   FOLLOW-UP: _____
   NAME: _____   TITLE: _____   SOURCE: _____
   RESULTS: _____

9. PH # _____   CO: _____   FOLLOW-UP: _____
   NAME: _____   TITLE: _____   SOURCE: _____
   RESULTS: _____

10. PH # _____   CO: _____   FOLLOW-UP: _____
    NAME: _____   TITLE: _____   SOURCE: _____
    RESULTS: _____

applications of current and former employees (references, former supervisors, coworkers, etc.). Students interested in research will want to check books and magazines for the authors of articles and reference works on the topics they are researching, as well as directories of companies involved in those fields commercially. Job seekers will want to pay attention to business articles about expansions, new ventures, and companies moving into their area, too.

When seeking names, don't forget your business card files, Rolodex, or address book. Some of those names will be the Priority Contacts you are seeking. Many more will be sources who might give you the names of priority contacts they know. Newspapers, magazines, news broadcasts, trade publications, and periodicals can often yield a variety of names of prospects, employers, executives, entrepreneurs, or others who may either be Priority Contacts, or give you names of those who are. Friends, relatives, and neighbors can be good sources of names, particularly when you are seeking domestic help, repair people, doctors, dentists, lawyers, etc.

The more names you need, the more resources you must develop. If you are in sales or any business where you must constantly generate new leads for customers or clients, you will want to keep an eye out for additional names or sources of prospects (Priority Contacts). If on the other hand you are only interested in a discount on one Sony Walkman, your local Yellow Pages will list all the resources you need.

Step 4: Prepare Your Telesearch Lists

If you need to make only a few calls for quick information, the Priority Call Planner (Figure 1) will be more than sufficient for planning and keeping track of each call. If however you must conduct an extensive Telesearch involving many calls for the same purpose, a list will help you stay organized and make all of those calls a lot faster. Use whatever resources you can find to prepare a Telesearch List of Priority Contacts (see Figure 7):

Space is provided at the top of the Telesearch List to record the date you make your calls, paging order, the purpose of the

Telesearch, and—if the list is used by others—the name of the caller, too. You can list ten calls in advance on a single page using lines provided for phone number (Ph #), company (Co), Priority Contact (Name), and Title. Make a note of where you got the name (Source). If for some reason you fail to reach your priority contact, make a note (Follow-up) if you leave a message, or if and when you should call back yourself. Extra space is also provided to note the Results of each call. If you need more space, keep a legal pad or Priority Call Planner beside your Telesearch Lists for recording more detailed information.

Many computer software packages are offered today that allow you to call up information about Priority Contacts on your computer screen, and prepare a Telesearch List from your data base. Some of the more advanced telemarketing systems not only prepare your lists for you, but actually dial for you too. Some automatically skip over busy signals and no answers so the telemarketer spends all his or her time talking with prospects. Although there are powerful advantages to such technology, it does raise the expense of telemarketing considerably. I prefer a printed list to working with a computer screen so I can scribble notes, etc., then transfer those notes to the computer after completing my calls.

Many sales departments, telemarketing operations, and market research organizations will use their own forms for call sheets. You can also use a legal pad. The Telesearch List shown in Figure 7 allows you to record the minimum amount of contact information you will want in front of you before making your calls. Be as elaborate as you wish, but don't get so bogged down in logistics, technology, and information that you spend more time compiling data than making your calls.

A Telesearch List is a time-saver.

If you list your calls in advance, you can complete twelve to fifteen calls (or more) in one hour.

If you don't have a prepared list, and have to look up each person to call before dialing, you will only complete four to six calls per hour. A Telesearch List not only helps improve productivity with your phone time (*by at least 200 to 300 percent*), it also helps increase your effectiveness on the phone with each call.

It is easier to maintain a high level of enthusiasm when you proceed immediately from one call to the next without pausing in between.

If on the other hand you must stop calling to look up every name and number, you will then have to "get yourself up" all over again for each call you make.

Group your outbound calls together, so you can enthusiastically complete five to ten in a row without pausing, and you will significantly improve your powers of INSTANT INFLUENCE with each call.

If you will be making a lot of calls to more than one classification of Priority Contacts, prepare different Telesearch Lists for each type. Maintain a separate list of sources who can furnish names of Priority Contacts. Label each list according to the type of contacts and project (Purpose) so you can file them for future reference, should you be involved in a similar project or need to reach the same people again. As you compile your Telesearch List of priority contacts, ask yourself . . .

Does my Priority Contact really have the authority to do what I need, or should I begin with someone higher up in the organization I plan to call?

If you have any doubts whatsoever the answer is probably yes. People will always find it easier to refer you down to one of their employees, rather than up to the boss. *Unless you are trying to recruit an individual with particular skills at a specific level*, you will almost always get better results if you start with Priority Contacts at the highest level possible (within reason of course).

Trade directories almost never give the names of lower level employees, but most will list the names of owners, presidents, vice presidents, and other key management personnel. If you cannot find the name of the person you need to contact from any of your resources, call the office of the executive in charge of the appropriate department in your target company, and ask his assistant for the name you need:

Assistant: "Mr. Thompson's office. This is Nita Beauchamp. May I help you?"

Caller: "I sure hope so. I understand you can tell me who is now your regional sales manager in Houston, Texas."

Be sure to include your Priority Contacts' first or given names on your Telesearch Lists so you can personalize your calls. We'll demonstrate in the next chapter how asking for someone by his or her given name helps you gain instant access to decision makers and avoid prescreening, too.

The size of your Telesearch Lists ultimately depends upon what you wish to accomplish. The best advice I can give here is to play the numbers.

Plan to make enough calls to be absolutely certain of achieving all of your objectives.

I'd want at least five competitive bids if I were seeking a discount or were involved in any kind of comparative shopping for the lowest prices. In order to be sure of obtaining five bids, I'd probably list seven to ten Priority Contacts on a Teleseasrch List, to allow for busy signals, numbers no longer in service, and those who may be out of pocket when I call. Job seekers usually average one interview for every ten calls they make, so they should list at least one hundred (or more) potential employers if they want to line up at least ten interviews in five to ten days.

If you have a staff preparing lists for three- to five-minute phone calls by your telemarketing department, plan on listing at least twelve to twenty names for each hour a professional telemarketer will spend on the phone. If conversations will be more lengthy or complex, shorten the lists accordingly. More is usually better than less.

Most professionals would rather complete an assignment with names left over than run out of people to call before achieving their objectives.

In the beginning you will need larger Teleseasrch Lists to guarantee your success, because as a beginner you will make natural mistakes. The more calls you make, the more experience you will gain, and the more effective you will eventually become with each call. As your phone skills improve, you will need to plan fewer calls to guarantee success.

Step 5: Practice Your Power Openers and Rebuttals Before Calling

Once your Telesearch List is prepared, and you know whom you will be calling, you will then want to plan your calls ahead of time as discussed in Chapter 1. Before writing out your Power Opener, you should know that there are basically two types of approaches you can choose from: direct and indirect. A Power Opener using a direct approach would go like this:

> **Caller: Jim, this is John Truitt at Telestar Inc. What's the lowest price you can give me on a case of Number Twelve Widgets?"**

In the above example, I am asking Jim for a discount, point-blank. I could use an indirect approach to achieve the same result.

> **"Jim, this is John Truitt at Telestar Inc. Who do you know who could give me the lowest price on a case of Number Twelve Widgets?"**

The indirect approach would almost always be followed by anyone seeking the name of Priority Contacts when talking to sources anyway. It is quite effective when used on Priority Contacts whom you wish to motivate to assist you without applying any direct pressure at all:

> "Gosh, John, we sell widgets ourselves, and I'm sure our manager would give you a very attractive discount for buying a whole case."

The above tactic can be particularly effective for someone who is not a retailer, but wants a wholesale price anyway. While the direct approach might have raised questions about my authority to receive a discount, the indirect approach deflects the contact's attention away from my qualifications, while he assures me that his firm can fulfill my needs (so I won't call someone else). There are numerous applications for the indirect approach in sales, recruiting, charity work, market research, comparative shopping, etc.

If you are enthusiastic when describing the type of person or assistance you want, those who fit the description will be inclined to identify themselves voluntarily.

Just like the sales pro who enthusiastically speaks in the third person to draw mental pictures his or her prospects will want to be in, you can use an enthusiastic indirect approach to "reverse" a Priority Contact into helping you achieve your goals.

A direct approach is only used when you <u>know</u> you are talking to a Priority Contact.

> **Caller: "Jim, this is John Truitt. I know you've done a lot of business with the XYZ Company. What can you tell me about how they pay their bills?"**

If you have any doubts as to whether the person you are talking to is a source or a Priority Contact, use an indirect approach.

> **Caller: "Jack, this is John Truitt. I'm trying to get some information about the XYZ Company, and was hoping you could give me some help. Who do you know who does business with XYZ, and might be able to tell me about how they handle their accounts payable?"**

You will probably use the indirect approach more often when Telesearching for information, and the direct approach for arranging appointments and influencing decisions. Later on we'll also discuss a variety of ways to combine both the direct and indirect approaches in the same phone call to get the results you want.

Since a Telesearch is basically a lot of priority calls grouped together for the same purpose, it may help to use the left side of a single Priority Call Planner (Figure 1) or legal pad to plan your calls in advance and list the materials or information you will need to have near the phone. Note first the purpose of the call and the questions you will ask, along with whatever questions or objections you might expect to hear from those you will be calling. Then write out an effective Power Opener, and prepare rebuttals to handle any questions or objections you might reasonably expect from Priority Contacts.

We have already discussed the advantages of getting to the point immediately to gain the Priority Contact's attention. As stated earlier, your Power Opener should introduce yourself, indicate the purpose of your call, and finish with a question to establish immediate control of the conversation. Often as not, you may either choose the most important of your questions to ask in your Power Opener, or actually phrase the purpose of your call in the form of your opening question. There are many times when you will want to use a forced response question or choice of two:

Caller: "Mr. Johnson, this is Billy Morris. I need to ask you some questions about your new telecommunications systems for our high school physics class. Should I stop by your office later this week? Or do you have a minute to answer a couple of quick questions on the phone?"

See how the forced-response question is used here to persuade the contact to talk now? If the caller had simply begun the discussion by asking if the contact had a couple of minutes to talk, he might have been refused. But when offered an option of a formal visit by appointment as opposed to continuing a present telephone conversation a little longer, most will choose the latter to save time and trouble. The same Teletactic can be useful when requesting product literature or any other information, too.

Caller: "Do I need to visit your offices personally to pick up the information I need, or can you have someone mail it to me?"

Here again (unless they are salespeople trying to attract customers into their showrooms), most Priority Contacts would rather have their secretaries mail information to inquirers than spend a lot of time with strangers visiting their offices. We've already discussed how forced-response questions can help arrange appointments. They will also help you influence decisions.

> **Caller: "Should I phone the home office, or do you have the authority to quote a discount price yourself?"**

Regardless of the approach you use or the type of questions you ask . . .

Always phrase the initial question in your Power Opener to encourage a positive response.

The indirect approach is by far the most useful for anyone doing any kind of recruiting, because it naturally helps you either obtain referrals or recruit the Priority Contact on the spot.

> **Caller: "Who is the most successful computer sales rep you know?"**
>
> **"Who would know the name of a reliable plumber who works cheap?"**
>
> **"I wondered if your daughter might have any friends in the neighborhood or at school who would be interested in babysitting this Friday night for $6.00 per hour?"**
>
> **"Jack, this is Bill Thompson. I'm involved in a very important executive search for a vice president of finance who is a CPA with twenty years of experience in the chemical industry. Who do you know who might be interested in an excellent opportunity with the highest paying company in the industry?"**

"Who do you know who . . ." is just as effective in sales, fund-raising, or when seeking public speakers, too.

"Mary, this is Ed Taylor. Who do you know who might be interested in saving as much as 40 percent on a brand new fax machine?"

"Bill, this is Mary Smith with Help the Homeless. I wondered if you might know any successful entrepreneurs like yourself who would be proud to have the names of their businesses publicly listed as sponsors for such a worthwhile cause?"

"George, this is Janice. Who do you know who could give an authoritative lecture on foreign relations to our group, without expecting to be paid a fortune in speaker's fees?"

There are times when, as mentioned earlier, you may wish to switch from the indirect approach to a more direct approach.

"How about your business, Bill. Shouldn't your firm be a sponsor, too?"

"I think you ought to recommend yourself for this opportunity, Jack. You're not only a CPA, but you've been the controller for that little chemical company for quite a while. Wouldn't you be interested in a major promotion where you could earn a lot more money, too?"

There are many ways to combine both the direct and indirect approaches in any given situation. If you start with a direct approach, a good rule to remember is . . .

Whenever a direct approach fails to achieve the results you want, switch to an indirect approach to get referrals.

Regardless of the purpose of your call, you will want to prepare rebuttals in advance, so you will be ready for any questions or objections you might get on the phone from contacts.

In order to feel confident and fully prepared for anything,

write out the ten worst questions or most difficult objections you could possibly run into.

Then, as explained in Chapter 1, prepare in advance satisfactory answers that end in questions to help you regain control of the conversation. Below are a few examples of the most common questions or objections you might run into when conducting a Telesearch for various kinds of information, with sample rebuttals that should give you more ideas of your own. Remember, these are sample responses, not a dialogue or an entire discussion. Although you will want to learn them all, use only one to three rebuttals (at most) in any one conversation.

Question: "How did you get my name?"

Rebuttal: "Can we just say I'm resourceful and leave it at that?"

Objection: "I'm not interested."

Rebuttal: "This doesn't require any interest at all, Mr. Johnson, just a couple of minutes of your courtesy. Should I plan on stopping by your office tomorrow, or can you take a minute on the phone to help me finish now?"

Question: "Why should I help you?"

Rebuttal: "I don't know, call it common courtesy if you wish. Can you think of any logical reason why you shouldn't?"

Objection: "I can't think of anyone who fits that description."

Rebuttal: "Well, I do appreciate your trying. Can you think of anyone I might call who would know the kind of person I'm looking for?"

Objection: "Put your request in writing through the proper channels."

Rebuttal: "That's fine with me, but I thought you would appreciate saving the expense of having your staff handle a formal request when a quick answer from you over the phone is all I really need. Do you prefer answering letters or can you deal with this now?"

Objection: "It's against company policy to give out that kind of information."

Rebuttal: "Oh, I don't want to cause any problems. What can you tell me without getting into trouble?"

or

"I can certainly appreciate the need for uniform policies and procedures. Can you tell me who sets the policies governing this kind of request?"

Objection: "I really don't wish to talk about it at all. Can we just say good-bye?"

Rebuttal: "OK, Ms. King, but before we get off the line, can you think of anyone I could call who might have a few dollars, some used clothing, or canned goods to share with the homeless families we're trying to help?"

Objection: "I don't have time."

Rebuttal: "Oh, I am sorry for calling at an inconvenient time. Will you have a couple of minutes to talk tomorrow morning, or should I call back this afternoon?"

or

"I know what you mean, because I'm kind of pressed for time myself. That's why I thought a quick phone call would help us both. Would you like me to call back later, or can you take a break to answer a couple of brief questions now?"

Objection: "That information is confidential."

Rebuttal: "I beg your pardon, I must not have phrased my question properly. I'm not interested in anything classified or top secret, I just wanted to know . . . ?"

Objection: "I never give strangers the names of my friends as referrals."

Rebuttal: "I don't blame you for looking out for your friends. Do you have any close friends who might appreciate getting inside information about a fantastic opportunity like this first, before someone else gets wind of it?"

Objection: "Give me your phone number, and I'll ask around. If anyone is interested I'll tell them to give you a call."

Rebuttal: "That's very kind of you to offer, but I wouldn't want you to spend your time doing my job. Besides, I'm so pressed for time I need to talk to someone today. Who is the first person you would ask if you were me?"

Whenever you are asking for names or referrals, you will manage your time more effectively and get more names if you avoid leaving a number as requested in the last example above. Others will never care as much about the project you are involved in as you do. Even though they may mean well when offering to pass your number around, they have their own priorities. Rather than put yourself in a position where you have to wait for others to act, ask your source to give you the phone numbers of the people he or she would ask, and complete those calls yourself.

Did you notice how virtually all of the rebuttals shown in the above examples began with indications of agreement (the Reverse) and ended with questions (Truitt's Law)? Can you see how Teletactics like these really will help you avoid arguments, control conversations, and achieve your objectives faster?

Although you will probably never need more than one to three rebuttals in any one conversation, you will want to develop and practice rebuttals to as many questions or objections as you might logically expect to hear. All are important, but . . .

You will most definitely want to be ready for the first question, statement, or objection the Priority Contact raises when you call.

Most people will be occupied doing something when you call. Instead of answering the phone with their minds blank, many will still be thinking about whatever they were doing when the phone rang.

The Priority Contact's first question is usually a delaying ploy to put you off for a second while he collects his thoughts.

You want to be sure to have an answer prepared in advance, so you may handle this first obstacle smoothly and move on toward controlling the conversation. Since you have no way of knowing in advance which question or objection you will hear first, you will need to practice all your rebuttals ahead of time.

The better you know your rebuttals, the less you will need them.

Effective use of rebuttals makes it easier to maintain control of conversations and actually avoid many of the questions or objections you might otherwise hear.

Write an effective Power Opener that will help you get to the point and establish immediate control of the conversation. Go over the questions and objections you might expect to receive on the phone and prepare rebuttals that sound logical and natural to you. Practice saying them out loud until you feel comfortable and can use them smoothly. If you are training professional pollsters, researchers, telemarketers, or others who will make outbound calls regularly for your organization, have them role-play their Power Openers and rebuttals until they know them by heart before allowing them on the phones.

Practice beforehand and keep your notes by the phone when calling so you will be prepared for anything.

Step 6: Use Your Best Phone Skills to Complete All Calls

I'm sure the Power Openers and rebuttals discussed so far seem kind of dry and lifeless in print. To make them sound genuinely persuasive, you must use a smiling, enthusiastic Telestyle. As stated earlier, the telephone offers a unique opportunity for one party to create the mood of the entire conversation in an instant. If you are friendly and cheerful, people on the other end of the phone line will want to be cooperative.

Knowing the Priority Contact's first or given name before calling allows you to assume familiarity from the very beginning. Unless protocol demands formality, or you are a child or teenager calling an adult, address the priority contact as an equal, one on one, without using "Mr." or "Ms." Such formal courtesies are proper for answering business phones, but when you are the caller, you want to avoid formalities that might make you sound like a stranger or underling, so you can get to the point immediately in a friendly manner. Address the Priority Contact by his or her first name as one professional to another, as if you should already be friends.

You need not rely upon someone else's name to get the results you want if you sound confident on the phone.

Smiling, assuming familiarity, speaking with enthusiasm, and using Teletactics effectively will help you project confidence during every conversation, and reap the benefits of INSTANT INFLU- ENCE immediately with friends and strangers alike. Remember . . .

Although people will never catch every word in your Power Openers or rebuttals, they will be influenced by <u>how</u> you communicate your sincerity and enthusiasm over the phone.

Most will be inclined to help you without ever realizing why. Review Chapter 1 before making your calls to remind you of all the skills that count. Keep a copy of the Call Review Checklist (Figure 2) beside you when making your calls, to be sure you use your best phone skills with each and every call. As stated earlier, you will succeed if you make up your mind to give each call your very best effort, and don't quit trying until you reach your goals.

Step 7: Get Something from Every Call

Don't be afraid to ask for help when Telesearching for information. If you communicate with a friendly, cheerful Telestyle, most people will be glad to answer questions and give you referrals when asked. Whether you are planning five calls or fifty, make sure each call you make is productive.

Use at least two or three rebuttals before you give up on the primary purpose of the call.

If you cannot get the results or information you need from the Priority Contact, ask for referrals or names of sources who may know the kind of person you are seeking. If you cannot obtain a name or other lead during the initial phone call, set up a time to call back later to see if your contact has anything for you then.

If you run into repeated objections or negative responses, it's probably you, not them.

Loosen up and smile. Remember to maintain a friendly, positive mental attitude when making your calls, and never allow any rudeness by another person to make you lose it and thereafter ruin your whole day's calls. If you keep a good attitude, you will be alert for opportunities on the phone, and it will be easier to implement the strategies, tactics, and skills discussed here to get at least something from every call. All those "somethings" add up to a significant record of accomplishments by the end of a Telesearch.

Telesearch The Universe Person to Person

You can Telesearch as far and wide as you wish through long distance. In the future, you may even be able to call space stations. Customers, vendors, prospects, employers, employees, and a variety of information sources around the world may be contacted in an instant by phone. If you know the person you will be calling as well as his or her habits of availability, by all means save as much money as you can with discount services or by dialing direct. If however you are calling someone you do not know . . .

Person-to-person saves long distance costs.

AT&T's operator-assisted person-to-person service is actually a lot cheaper than discount services or dialing direct if you make a lot of long-distance calls to people you do not know. If you dialed direct, you would have to pay for every connection, discussion with secretaries, and all the time you waste on hold, too. If you use person-to-person, you will only pay for the actual time spent talking to your Priority Contact—and you can leave a message for free if the party you are calling is not available.

Although the operator will give a "call operator 15" (or whatever her special number is), most people in business consider it a professional courtesy to pay for return calls themselves. This means that many of your actual conversations will cost you nothing. Some job seekers with limited funds wait until they know it is lunch time in the area they are calling, and then call their out-of-town prospects person-to-person to save on long-distance charges.

Another advantage to using person-to-person for a Telesearch is that you may call for someone by title only, if you don't have a name. The AT&T operator will even help you find out the name of your Priority Contact if you ask ahead of time:

Caller: "Operator, I'd like to make a person-to-person call to the vice president of finance at area code 222, 555-1231. And would you find out this person's name for me too, please?"

Your calls will often be put through to decision makers faster, because AT&T operators don't fool around answering a lot of screening questions from secretaries or receptionists, either. Once you learn your Priority Contact's schedule, you may direct-dial in the future to reduce your long-distance expenses even more.

Directories of companies that use toll-free 800 numbers should be found in your public library. You can also dial 1-800-555-1212 (for a small charge) to learn if the company or organization you wish to call has a toll-free number that you can dial from your area code. I believe in economy when it comes to long-distance phone calls, but it pays to bear in mind . . .

Any long-distance call is cheaper than a visit, faster, and by far easier to use, than any other method of two-way communications.

You need neither license nor passport to call anyone on the planet by phone. You don't have to pack your bags or wear a tie either. 800 numbers and person-to-person can offer affordable means of expanding your small business at home into an international operation in an instant. How you capitalize upon that instant will ultimately be determined by your successful use of effective Power Openers and rebuttals.

If You Avoid Distractions, You Leave Nothing to Chance

We have already discussed how the first few seconds of any phone call are by far the most important.

Anything that might conceivably cause the Priority Contact's attention to stray momentarily from the purpose of your call should be deleted from your Power Opener.

Small talk or any mention of previous correspondence or a mutual acquaintance is a needless distraction, and it will leave you wide open to disrupting questions, statements, or objections. Mentioning advance mailings in the beginning of a conversation can cause real problems.

"What letter? I haven't seen any résumé! You sent a query letter to me? Hold on . . . Marieeeeee! We get a lot of junk mail. Whom did you send it to? What address? I don't have time to look at everything coming in on our fax machine. When did you send it? Send another, and we'll call you back if we're interested."

Phone first for INSTANT INFLUENCE.

If you call first, *before mailing flyers, résumés, or query letters*, you will avoid any distractions that might prevent you from getting to the point immediately in your Power Opener. You will not only achieve more during the call itself, but if you must send something to the Priority Contact afterward . . .

Written correspondence will receive much more attention if it is sent to follow up a phone call.

If you learn to rely upon good phone skills rather than advance mailings to help you make successful phone calls to strangers, you can save a lot of time and money, too. Although substantial, the savings in costs of word-processing, printing, paper, and postage are really insignificant when compared to the days or even weeks you will save by Telesearching to reach your ultimate goals.

Saying you were referred by someone you don't really know very well can be risky.

> Callee: "Who? I've never heard of him. Why does she keep giving people my name? How is old Bill? How many kids do they have now? Do they still play backgammon? You tell him I'm not helping anybody until he pays me for . . ."

Meaningless small talk in your Power Opener can backfire with strangers.

> Callee: "How am I doing? My wife left me six months ago with five kids on my hands. I'm broke, and about to lose my job if I don't quit wasting time answering stupid questions. How the hell do you think I'm doing?"

Small talk and name-dropping are fine with people you know, but not with strangers. These little tidbits may seem humorous here, but they can destroy your productivity on the telephone in an instant by causing you to lose control of conversations. You can avoid all of these needless distractions with a Telesearch Plan, good phone skills, and a brief, effective Power Opener.

Summary

Here, again, are the seven basic steps of a successful Telesearch Plan:

1. Develop a strategy to reach your specific goals.
2. Profile your Priority Contacts.
3. Develop your resources.
4. Prepare your Telesearch lists.

5. Practice your Power Openers and rebuttals before calling.
6. Use your best phone skills to complete all calls.
7. Get something from every call.

Success is virtually guaranteed if you plan your Telesearch as shown here, because you will leave very little to chance. The next three chapters will help you follow your plan to overcome front office defenses, get through to decision makers, arrange appointments quickly, and influence important decisions instantly. You will no longer have to wait for sluggish mail services or actions by third parties, who would prefer to pursue their own priorities instead of yours.

Good phone skills, effective Teletactics, and a reliable Telesearch Plan will combine to give you instant access to all kinds of key people who can help you reach your ultimate goals faster. As the old saying goes . . .

If you plan your work and work your plan, success is inevitable.

6

PHONE TACTICS
FOR INSTANT ACCESS
TO DECISION MAKERS

The ability to penetrate front office defenses to reach key executives and other important people is a valuable skill, anyone can learn and use. Getting through third party screeners will not only save time and trouble on any kind of project, but it is the key to success with virtually any assignment.

The power to influence decisions depends first and foremost upon one's ability to reach the real decision makers.

This chapter will focus on tactics for avoiding or overcoming screening procedures. The remaining chapters will discuss ways to capitalize upon this access either to arrange definite appointments or to influence a variety of decisions on the spot.

Professionalism Is the Key to Instant Access

Those who have problems penetrating front office defenses usually blame secretaries, receptionists, switchboard operators, and other screeners for their own failures. Secretaries are not monsters. Most in fact try to handle their jobs with pleasant efficiency.

The caller who starts out poorly, fails to control conversations, or reacts incorrectly to perfectly normal questions invariably finds it difficult or impossible to penetrate the simplest screening procedures.

Screening questions are part of any executive secretary's job. Having taught the skills myself, I can attest to the fact that secretaries can be excellent screeners—*when callers allow them to be*. Many callers stumble or hesitate over the simplest questions. Most tell the secretary too much, while others get flustered, angry, or indignant. Those who argue or get emotional will always fail, because just like the others, their *lack of professionalism* warns secretaries to screen their calls more closely.

Someone (I wish I knew who) once said: "A 'professional' is one who knows what to do, what to say, how to do it, and how to say it in any conceivable situation."

Anyone who divulges unnecessary information or gets flustered or argumentative with a secretary or receptionist obviously fails to meet the above standard. Such amateurish behavior alerts even the dullest screener that the caller should be examined closely before being allowed to talk to the boss. The professional, on the other hand, will often have his or her calls put through immediately, without hearing any screening questions at all.

If you prepare in advance what to say and how to say it, you will sound like a professional—the kind whose calls should always be put through to Priority Contacts without delay.

Although I've mentioned it many times, it would be impossible to overemphasize the critical importance of using a smiling, cheerful, genuinely friendly Telestyle when penetrating front office defenses.

Smile when you speak, so that the tone of your voice implies both your familiarity with procedures and your confidence that your call will be put through without delay.

Then don't clutter up this confident, self-assured first impression with a lot of words.

Use a Quick Power Opener with Screeners

If the person answering the phone is not your Priority Contact, you may correctly assume that he or she is a screener. His job is to screen calls to save the boss's time. Your job is to penetrate those screening procedures as quickly as possible to save *your* time. A simple, brief Power Opener will save everyone's time:

Caller: "This is <u>John Truitt</u> for <u>Jim Johnson</u>. Is he in?"

This is all you need to say if someone else answers the phone when you are calling a Priority Contact. Why?

A simple, quick Power Opener tells the secretary all she really needs to know to complete the call, and focuses her attention upon answering your question, instead of screening the call.

Your friendly manner, coupled with enthusiasm and brevity, will make it seem natural to put your call through.

Secretary: "Yes, he is, Mr. Truitt. Will you hold for a moment while I connect you, please?"

The Power Opener shown above may cause some secretaries and receptionists to stumble out of habit.

"Yes, may I tell him who's—oops, you already gave me your name didn't you, Mr. Truitt?"

Just laugh along with her and seize the opportunity for a brief bond of kindred spirit:

Caller: "It sounds like things are as hectic in your office [chuckling] as they are in mine. Is Jim available now?"

Some screeners may recover enough to ask a question, but this kind of friendly exchange will almost always result in your call being put through without delay.

Be prepared to adjust your Power Opener to respond to the screener's introduction.

If, for instance, a business phone is answered this way . . .

Secretary: "Mr. Johnson's office, may I help you?"

Smile, assume familiarity (as if you already are on friendly terms), and respond the same way the Priority Contact's friends and business acquaintances would respond:

Caller: "Yes, this is John Truitt. Is he in?"

If the phone answerer gives his or her own name as well as the Priority Contact's . . .

"Mr. Johnson's office. This is Judy. May I help you?"

Alter your Power Opener to include a friendly use of the screener's name:

Caller: "Hi, Judy. This is John Truitt. Is he in?"

Being alert to what the screener says in his or her introduction can be used (with a friendly Telestyle) to make you sound like someone who has been calling that office for years. This assumption of familiarity eliminates most screening procedures instantly.

Callers Have the Edge

Even though one might think the secretary is on location and in control, the advantage really lies with the caller.

The caller has had time to prepare for the call, is mentally alert, and is ready to seize control of the conversation—which he initiates in the opening seconds.

The secretary, receptionist, switchboard operator, or other screener will probably be occupied with something else when the phone rings. It will take at least a second or two for him or her to focus full mental concentration upon handling the call.

A brief but effective Power Opener like "This is John Truitt for Jim Johnson. Is he in?" takes *only three seconds* to say. This means that, by the time the secretary can fully concentrate, you will already have established control of the conversation with your first question: "Is he [she] in?" Since the time frame for reaction is so brief, most secretaries rely upon first impressions rather than explanations to determine whether or not to ask screening questions.

If, during the first few seconds of the conversation, you sound friendly and confident, as if you expect your call to be put through immediately—it will be, if you also remember to seize control with a question.

Your friendly nature combined with an air of confident professionalism will make you sound like someone whose name is probably already on the boss's PC list (see Chapter 4). Asking a question like "Is he in?" keeps the secretary momentarily off balance so she has no time to think things through, much less ask questions of her own.

The best way to avoid questions is to ask questions.

I cannot overemphasize the importance of using questions when dealing with screeners on the telephone. If you control conversations with questions from the very beginning, you will have no real problems with screening procedures. Remember the Reverse, Truitt's Law, and the Politician's Ploy for those secretaries (possibly my own readers) who are better than average screeners.

How to Breeze Through Screening Questions with Ease

Some screeners will not be swayed by a Power Opener and will persist with asking questions of their own. Since you have no way of knowing in advance which ones will ask questions . . .

You must be ready for questions every time you pick up the telephone.

Unless you already know the secretary who answers the phone, or you are calling a head of state, the Pope, or a famous celebrity . . .

You will probably not want to tell the screener what your call is about.

With a major public figure, you will doubtless have to explain your reason for calling. But you will definitely not want to discuss the purpose of your call with any third party if you are engaged in any kind of investigative reporting, recruiting, sales, marketing, business development, fund-raising effort, political project, or job search. Although great sources of information . . .

Secretaries are not the real decision makers.

Even if you were to give the secretary the full sales pitch for your product or services, she will most likely reduce your brilliant presentation to something like "There's a guy on the phone trying to sell something," or "Do you want to talk to this lady about a job?" Remember . . .

No one cares as much about the purpose of your call as you do.

Fortunately there are only so many questions secretaries and receptionists can logically ask during those brief seconds when they answer the phone. If you are alert and prepared, with your Power Opener and rebuttals practiced in advance, you can seize control of those first few seconds with smooth rebuttals and questions of your own.

The entire conversation with a secretary or receptionist should last no longer than six to thirty seconds.

The most common questions or objections you are likely to hear are shown in the following pages, along with sample rebuttals to give you ideas for planning and practicing your own responses ahead of time.

You will seldom need to use more than <u>one to three rebuttals</u> <u>at most</u> during any one conversation, with even the best of screeners.

Review the section on screening calls in Chapter 4, to list the most likely questions to expect from secretaries. Several examples are given for the most common questions you will run into, so you may choose the kind of rebuttal that best suit your individual needs.

Rebuttals for Screening Questions

Question: "What company are you with?"
Rebuttal: "It's my own firm. Is he available now?"

or

"Just tell him it's John Truitt with Telestar Inc.—unless you can put me through now, please?"

or

"It's not that kind of call. Is he available now?"

Question: "May I tell him what your call is about?"
Rebuttal: "Sure, just tell him it's John Truitt, and would you tell him I'm holding, please?"

or

"Yes, it'll take about two minutes. Is he in?"

Question: "I really need to know the purpose of your call. Could you be more specific, please?"

Rebuttal: **"Sure, it's a professional matter, and I need to speak with him personally about it. Is he available now?"**

or

"Yes, I need to speak with him personally to save time clearing up a couple of questions on a professional matter. Can you connect me now, please?"

Question: "Does he know you?"

Rebuttal: **"Well, you won't put him on the spot if you just tell him I'm holding. Could you do that for me now, please?"**

or

"He shouldn't feel embarrassed if he doesn't recognize my name. Is he available now?"

or

"I wouldn't test his memory when you tell him I'm holding—unless you can put me through now, please?"

Question: "Will he know what your call is about?"

Rebuttal: **"Well, I've been trying to avoid spilling the beans until I could talk with him personally. Is he available, now?"**

or

"I'm trying to save us both some time. Can you put me through now, please?"

Question: "Is she expecting your call?"

Rebuttal: **"I seriously doubt if she is expecting to hear from me today, but I do need to speak with her right away. Can you connect me now, please?"**

Question: "What are you selling?"

or

"Will she know what products [or services] you wanted to talk about?"

Rebuttal: "You must be expecting someone else. Would you tell her that John Truitt is holding, please?"

Question: "I really need to know more about the nature of your call."

Rebuttal: "Certainly, there are just a couple of last minute questions I need to go over with her personally. Is she available now?"

Try not to lose patience with those who screen harder.

Question: "What kinds of questions did you wish to ask?"

Rebuttal: "I beg your pardon. Is there something wrong with his phone?"

Reply: "No, but as Mr. Johnson's executive assistant I am responsible for screening all of his calls."

Rebuttal: "Well, I'll be sure to tell him what a fine job you're doing, Judy, but I'll need to speak with him right away in order to finish on time. Can you connect me now, please?"

Objection: "I cannot process your call until you tell me what it's about."

Rebuttal: "Thanks for trying to help, but I'd better talk with him about this. Is he free now?"

or

"Listen, I really do appreciate your interest, but this is the kind of thing I need to go over with him personally. Does he know how long I've been kept waiting?"

If the screener keeps on giving you a hard time . . .

Caller: "I know you're trying to help, but I don't think I should discuss this with anyone until I've cleared it with her first. Would you rather take a message and have her call me back, or should I continue to hold?"

These rebuttals may appear evasive or argumentative in print, but remember—you will only be using one to three in any single conversation. Furthermore they will not sound that way on the phone if you maintain a cheerful, friendly attitude throughout the entire discussion.

The way you handle yourself makes a much greater impression than the words you use.

Use the shorter, quicker rebuttals first, before progressing to lengthier explanations, and don't fail to end each statement with a question to stay in control. It is perfectly ethical to be resourceful and use creative rebuttals, but . . .

Never lie to a screener, or say that it is a personal call, urgent, or an emergency unless it truly is.

Even if you do get past the secretary, the Priority Contact will be so enraged at you for lying that he or she will probably (with justification) hang up the phone and never speak to you again.

Record the Secretary's Name for Future Reference

Whenever you are given the name of a secretary, receptionist, switchboard operator, family member, etc., write it down on your Priority Call Planner or Telesearch List, so you can remember to use it the next time you call.

Caller: "Hi, Mary, this is John Truitt. Is Jim in?"

Using the secretary's first name in a friendly Power Opener implies instantly that you are familiar with his or her office. People are always pleased when callers remember their names. Most will assume they are supposed to know you, and will put your call through immediately to avoid embarrassment by having to admit they don't remember you.

Make this phenomenon work for you. Whenever you have a very important phone call, where you must eliminate any chance of not reaching the Priority Contact . . .

Call ahead of time to get the executive secretary's name from the receptionist, switchboard operator, or whoever answers the phone—*before* calling the Priority Contact.

Use the Letter Technique if you wish.

Caller: "Yes, I need to personalize a thank-you note to Jim Johnson's secretary, and wondered if you could tell me what name her friends call her, and give me the correct spelling, please?"

Usually you only need a secretary's name when you must leave absolutely nothing whatsoever to chance. Following the guidelines in this chapter will help you get through most of the screeners you will encounter without knowing their names. Still, if a secretary does give you a particularly hard time during your first call, you can use the Letter Technique afterward to learn his or her name, and call back a few days later with the personal Power Opener above. If that doesn't work . . .

Why Not Try an End Run?

A familiar Telestyle, good Power Openers, and smooth rebuttals will take care of well over 90 percent of the screeners you encounter on the phone, but nothing works all the time. Eventually you will run into a secretary or executive assistant who will simply not put your call through to his or her boss. As a last resort . . .

Before giving up completely, try calling early in the morning or after hours when—it's worth a try—your Priority Contact may be in, but the secretary is not.

Often your Priority Contact will answer the phone himself.

If the Priority Contact Is No Longer There . . .

Occasionally the screener will inform you that your Priority Contact is no longer with the company or at the number you called. If you want to talk to whoever is in the same position . . .

> **Caller: "Well, I guess I'd better update my records. Can you tell me who has that job, now? Do you know her first name or what her friends call her? Can you connect me with her office now, please?"**

If you still want to talk to the particular individual you were originally calling . . .

> **"Do you have a phone number where I can reach him now?"**

"Would You Like to Hold or Leave a Message?"

Personally, I'd rather hold for a minute than leave a message, because at that point I'm only a minute away from completing my call to my Priority Contact.

Leaving a message always introduces at least an outside risk of not having your message returned.

However, I do not like to hold longer than a minute.

> **Caller: "Yes, I can hold for one minute, but you won't forget me, will you?"**

Of course as stated earlier, nothing works all the time, but experience has taught me that if I make a point of asking not to be forgotten, the employee who put me on hold will be conscientious enough to keep his or her promise. If after a minute the secretary says the Priority Contact is still on another line, you will then have to decide whether or not to continue holding. Unless immediate contact is urgent, you should probably go ahead and leave a message. If you feel you should continue to hold . . .

> Caller: "Well, I can hold a little longer, but please check back with me if it looks like it will take longer than another minute. Can you do that for me, please?"

If a secretary, screener or even a family member (when you are calling someone at home) tells you your Priority Contact is busy, tied up, in conference, on the showroom floor, or otherwise occupied . . .

Respect the value of your Priority Contact's time.

Unless it is an emergency or extremely urgent, leave a message. Otherwise the Priority Contact will begin his or her end of the conversation irritated with you for the interruption.

If you let Priority Contacts call back when it is convenient for them, you will have a far better chance of influencing the ensuing conversation the way you want to.

The Right Way to Leave a Message

Many secretaries are taught (as explained in Chapters 2 and 4) to continue the screening process when taking messages. Instead of lowering your guard when leaving a message . . .

Continue to control the conversation with questions.

> Secretary: "I'm sorry, but Mr. Johnson isn't in [is tied up, in a meeting, etc.] right now. Would you like to leave a message?"
>
> **Caller: "OK, do you have a pen and paper?"**
>
> Secretary: "Yes I do. May I have the number you're calling from?"
>
> **Caller: "Ask him to call John Truitt at 555-1335 before five o'clock this afternoon. Or if that's not convenient, he can**

call me this evening at 555-1833 between 6 and 9 p.m. Would you like to read those numbers back to me, please?"

Secretary: "Yes sir, that's John Truitt at 555-1335 before five o'clock this afternoon, or 555-1833 between six and nine o'clock tonight. Was there anything else you'd like me to tell him, Mr. Truitt?"

Caller: "No, but do you know when he'll receive the message?"

Secretary: "He should pick up his messages in about an hour."

Caller: "That will be fine. Thank you very much."

Remember . . .

If you don't ask questions, the screener will.

If you fail to control the message-taking sequence with questions of your own, you will find yourself answering a barrage of questions like "What company are you with?", "What is the call about?", "Does he know you?" etc. Little questions of your own like "Do you have a pen and paper?", "Can you read that back to me please?", and "Do you know when he'll receive the message?" will help you stay in control while the secretary is busy writing down information and trying to answer you. If you keep her busy like this, she will not have time to ask any screening questions of her own.

Giving alternate times and phone numbers when leaving messages should help you and your Priority Contact get together sooner, without playing phone tag all day long.

If your Priority Contact is out of town, ask for a number where he may be reached, or the time when he will be checking his messages.

If you are given a number, call person-to-person and let the AT&T operator deal with screening procedures for you. Otherwise, give the Priority Contact time to check his messages and call you back. As a rule . . .

You will connect with your Priority Contact faster, and

arouse less suspicion, if you leave a message rather than offer to call back later.

Don't be afraid to leave a message. Although there may be a risk of not having your call returned, most people try their best. A stranger who will not leave his name and number sends up a red flag. Next time you call, the secretary may screen you more closely than during the original call. If for some reason you cannot leave a phone number, leave a message offering a *brief explanation* to avoid suspicions, and inquire as to the best time to call your Priority Contact . . .

> **Caller: "Tell him John Truitt called, but since I'll be tied up this afternoon, I'll try to get back to him later myself. When would be the best time for me to catch him in the office?"**

There is nothing wrong with asking for the most convenient time to call, but . . .

Don't pump a secretary or assistant for a lot of information when calling his or her boss.

Secretaries are great sources of information *when you call them directly*, but they are very protective of the boss, and when you are trying to get through to him, asking a lot of questions can make you appear sneaky. This, of course, will destroy your professional image with the secretary.

When to Follow up Your Calls

Always give your Priority Contact enough time to return your calls before placing a follow-up call.

But don't wait indefinitely unless you were told it would take longer.

If you leave word in the afternoon, and your call is not returned by 9:45 the following morning, call again. If you leave a message in the morning which has not been returned, call back around 2:15 to 2:30 that afternoon.

Delaying follow-up on your afternoon calls until the next day allows more than enough time for a Priority Contact to receive a message and call you back. Waiting until 2:15 P.M. to follow up your morning calls should give your Priority Contact ample time to check his messages after lunch and call you back.

Those who do not return your calls should be called again. If for some reason the Priority Contact is still not available, leave another message. Then wait until just before lunch time the following day before calling those (if any) who have still not returned your calls. After that (unless it is extremely urgent) let it rest a couple of days rather than seem too pesky or anxious.

This procedure should help you get in touch with all the Priority Contacts you need to reach as quickly as possible, while remaining in control of your own schedule, too. If someone continues to ignore your messages, try calling before or after hours as mentioned earlier.

Use INSTANT INFLUENCE for Instant Access

You will not have any problems to speak of if you relax and enjoy your discussions with secretaries while letting your skills and tactics help you penetrate front-office defenses.

If you memorize your Power Opener and rebuttals, smile, speak with enthusiasm, control conversations with questions, maintain a positive mental attitude, and use the Reverse, Politician's Ploy, and Truitt's Law to handle difficult questions— <u>you will penetrate even the most strenuous of screening procedures in less than a minute!</u>

That's what I mean by "instant access." The tactics we've discussed so far will help you alone to create opportunities to reach the key people in any field. Now that you have learned how to reach anyone you want to instantly, the next chapter will help you capitalize immediately upon these opportunities to arrange definite appointments with Priority Contacts on your own.

7

HOW TO ARRANGE
IMPORTANT APPOINTMENTS
WITH ANYONE

I t is easy to set up a meeting with someone you know, but what about arranging appointments with high-level contacts you don't know? Imagine the unlimited opportunities for influence and profit if you could arrange face-to-face meetings with anyone, at any level, on your own terms? What might you or your organization accomplish if all doors were open—if instead of knowing the right people, all you needed were a name and phone number so you could contact any decision-maker quickly, and arrange an appointment on the spot?

The ability to arrange appointments with Priority Contacts whenever you want to will significantly improve your odds of success in any endeavor.

Budget Your Time for Maximum Productivity

Grouping your calls together will not only help you maintain an enthusiastic Telestyle, it will also make it easier to manage your phone time more efficiently. Obviously, if you want maximum productivity . . .

Budget the time to place your calls when you can reasonably expect to reach the most Priority Contacts.

Normally it is easier to reach executives in their offices on weekday mornings, instead of the afternoons. Many doctors should be called late in the mornings, after they have completed their hospital rounds, while a lot of practicing attorneys are easier to reach in the afternoons. Restaurant owners usually have more time to talk between 9:45 and 10:45 in the mornings, or after 2:15 in the afternoons. While nightclub owners and managers may be more accessible between 2 and 4 in the afternoons, late-night performers may not be coherent until after 12 noon.

If you have trouble reaching the president, owner, or executive in a firm during the regular work day, try calling forty-five minutes before or after normal business hours.

Many entrepreneurs and executives enjoy working alone before and after hours, when things are quiet, and often answer the phones themselves when no one else is around.

Most working adults are easier to reach at home on weekends and (unless they work a night shift) in the evenings during the week. We should all follow rules of common courtesy when phoning a Priority Contact at home.

Unless otherwise instructed, never call someone you don't know at home after 9 P.M., before 8 A.M. on weekdays, 10 A.M. on Saturdays, and 3 P.M. on Sundays.

Best times to call vary with occupations, the practice at different firms, and individual preference. But as a rule . . .

You will be more successful arranging appointments if you start your calls as early as Priority Contacts begin their work day.

Calling early will not only improve the odds of catching your Priority Contacts in their offices, it will also make it easier to set appointments, because they are still arranging their day's schedules. If you wait until later in the work day, many will be out of their offices or in meetings, etc.

We usually perform better on the phone in the mornings, because that is when we are more alert.

The more alert you are, the better your Telestyle, and the quicker you will respond with the right Teletactics and rebuttals to any questions or objections you run into on the phone.

Plan your phone time for maximum efficiency within your own schedule and work habits. If you prefer to complete your Telesearch calls in the mornings, as I do, prepare your Telesearch Lists the afternoon or evening before. Then you will be ready and able to complete at least twelve to fifteen calls in less than an hour the following morning. Budget time in the afternoons for follow-up calls, gathering information, obtaining referrals, and returning your own phone messages.

If you are in outside sales, plan your schedule to allow enough time each week for prospecting and arranging appointments for sales presentations by telephone. Most sales pros prepare their Telesearch Lists on Fridays or Saturdays, so they can arrange the following week's appointments by phone on Monday mornings, but each person's style and work habits are different.

Although quick calls for appointments are usually more successful in the morning, calls for information may be more appropriate later in the day, when people are more relaxed and won't mind lengthier discussions. If your Priority Contacts are more accessible in the afternoons or evenings, use the earlier hours to plan your calls in advance. Regardless of when you place your calls, heed the advice offered earlier and . . .

Be sure your Telesearch Lists are fully prepared in advance so you will not squander your most productive phone time with tasks that keep you off the telephone.

Once you begin placing your calls, try to work through your entire list as quickly as possible without interruptions. Even if you miss your Priority Contact with the first call, leave a message with alternate times and/or phone numbers to avoid playing phone tag in the future.

Once you have established a friendly dialogue with a Priority Contact, ask when he or she is usually available to receive calls. Then for future reference, write it down.

Be Prepared for Arranging Appointments

Have a calendar or your appointment book in front of you, of course, before placing your calls, so you may plan in advance the most convenient dates and times for arranging appointments (as far as your own schedule is concerned). If you are arranging appointments for someone else, be sure to ask for a selection of dates and times your client can be available for the meeting(s) you are trying to arrange. Then, write a Power Opener that helps you avoid distracting small talk and get to the point immediately.

Prepare a Power Opener that assumes familiarity and states who you are, why the appointment should be arranged, and ends by asking the Priority Contact which of two alternate times (ideal for you) is the most convenient for him or her to meet with you (or your client).

Unless you are a child calling an adult or a young adult calling a senior citizen at home, use the Priority Contact's first or given name when you know it. There are certain people—members of local government, royalty, national leaders, religious figures—whom you should always address as "Reverend," "Councilman," "Mayor,"

"Congressman," "Governor," "Senator," "Mr. President," or "Your Grace, Honor, Excellency, Royal Highness, Eminence," etc. Whenever you are unsure of how you should address such people, a quick preliminary call to his or her office (embassy, consulate, or chancery office) using the Letter Technique mentioned earlier will provide the answer . . .

"Yes, I'd like to personalize a letter to the Pope, and wondered if you could give me the correct mailing address along with guidelines for using the correct protocol in beginning my letter."

Using first or given names with everyone else will help you get to the point immediately and establish a friendlier rapport on the spot. Some Priority Contacts will probably think they ought to remember you, because of this instant familiarity, but isn't that why you want to arrange the meeting—so you can both get to know each other? If you do run across someone who prefers being addressed as Mr. or Ms., by all means do so. Removing such formality when you can will usually result in a friendlier, less rigid conversation.

"Who you are" may include no more than your name and (if it is a working call) the name of the company or organization you represent. Job hunters and those seeking auditions, tryouts, a talk show appearance, or an agent, etc. may also want to include in their Power Openers a few words describing their experience, ability, skills, or talent. Sales, marketing and business-development people, fund-raisers, political campaign workers, reporters, and entrepreneurs may also want to give a brief description of their organization or business as well. But don't get too long-winded in a Power Opener.

Save some facts about yourself or your organization with which to answer the Priority Contact's questions later.

When explaining why the appointment should be arranged . . .

Make the Priority Contact want to meet with you by enthusiastically describing some benefit to him or her for doing so.

Sales professionals have learned that the most appealing benefits are those that in some way help the prospect make or save money. Saving time, increasing sales, income, or profits, improving efficiency, productivity or effectiveness, lowering costs, improving quality control or a company's public image, attracting more customers, speeding delivery, saving or eliminating expenses, etc., are all the kinds of benefits that can affect a Priority Contact's wallet or job performance. The chance to learn something new or obtain information is another benefit one might use, as is the opportunity to perform charitable work or contribute to social programs that do some good. Ways to avoid hassles, improve one's life-style, have more leisure time—descriptions of these and many other benefits may help you obtain an appointment.

Enthusiasm creates a sense of urgency.

If you are not excited about meeting with your Priority Contact, why should he be excited—or even interested? Your enthusiasm should make the Priority Contact *want* to meet with you—to learn what all that urgency is about.

Focus your questions upon when you should meet rather than if you should meet.

Do not ask if a Priority Contact wants to meet with you. He will tell you if he doesn't. Instead, allow your friendly professionalism and enthusiasm to imply that, of course, the two of you should meet as soon as possible. Capitalize on this dynamic first impression immediately and end your Power Opener with a choice of two times to make it easier for your Priority Contact to say yes to a meeting.

Instead of questioning you, many of the people you call will immediately look at their calendars to see which of the two times you offered is best for them.

That is exactly how you want them to react. Naturally some others will ask questions or raise objections, but if just half your Priority Contacts agree to an appointment, think how far that will take you toward your goal. You can make it even easier to say yes if your first choices of two are fairly open:

Caller: "Could we get together in your office later on this week, or would the early part of next week be better for you?"

If the Priority Contact chooses either, that is a yes. Then continue using choices of two to narrow it down to a definite date and time:

"Fine. Should we say ten o'clock this Thursday morning, or would 1:30 Friday afternoon be more convenient for you?"

Regardless of when you agree to meet . . .

Get the appointment first, then go over the details.

I realize many job hunters and performers will want to know if there are openings first, but these questions are not necessary. No executive, employer, agent, or night club owner will agree to an employment interview or audition unless he or she has some opportunity in mind. If you ask outright, many employers will say they have no openings even when they do, because such information may be considered confidential—or they may be thinking of replacing unsatisfactory employees and don't want the word to get around.

Salespeople are taught to qualify their prospects first, but that is usually where they blow it on the phone, because prospects become irritated or bored with so many questions from strangers. By all means qualify your prospect before traveling to his or her office— *but do it after you have confirmed a definite appointment.* After all, if you can't arrange the appointment, all those other questions will be pointless anyway. If you learn something negative later, you can always cancel the appointment.

If you set the appointment first, you will have accomplished the purpose of your call.

This way, even if the call is interrupted and your Priority Contact has to get off the line, you will still have the appointment. You can always call him or his secretary later to obtain additional information or directions for finding their offices. Focus the conversation upon arranging the appointment first—the primary purpose of the call. It will save both your time and Priority Contact's.

When they're phoning long distance, some callers (particularly job seekers) may wish to alter their choices of two from time to place:

> **Caller: "Are you going to be in my area anytime soon, or do I need to come to New York?"**

This tactic is particularly useful for anyone hoping to have his travel expenses reimbursed by the Priority Contact or his company. If the Priority Contact says you should travel to his city, go ahead and confirm the date and time as discussed earlier, and then *if you feel his company should cover your travel expenses* . . .

> **"Ok, I'll be in your New York office at two o'clock next Thursday afternoon the fifth. Will your office make travel arrangements from your end, or should I handle it from here and turn in an expense voucher when I get there?"**

Also useful for consultants, this is simply a nicer way of confirming expense procedures before leaving on a trip for a new client or prospective employer.

Avoid small talk until after you have confirmed the appointment.

Small talk is fine when talking with friends and people you know, but keep it brief and it will improve your overall efficiency with these calls, too. Meaningless chatter from a stranger will invariably turn your Priority Contact off. In fact, I believe that pointless small talk accounts for the majority of failures salespeople experience when trying to arrange appointments with prospects. It simply wastes too much precious time, gives the Priority Contact a bad first impression, and allows him more leisure to realize he is talking to a stranger (obnoxious, too) with whom he may not want to waste any more of his time in a meeting.

Use a friendly, cheerful, enthusiastic Telestyle and keep the conversation focused upon arranging the appointment. Unnecessary small talk may cause you to lose control.

Examples of Power Openers and Rebuttals

The following examples of Power Openers (PO) for arranging appointments and sample rebuttals for questions and objections from Priority Contact should give you ideas for preparing your own.

Arranging TV and Radio Talk Show Appearances

PO: "Mary, this is Jim Johnson with XYZ Security. We thought you might like to invite one of our corporate officers to be a guest on your show to discuss tips for home security and answer questions from callers. Do you have a spot open this week, or is next week better for you?"

Objection: "I don't think home security is our kind of topic."

Rebuttal: "I realize it might be different, but a lot of your listeners are homemakers or senior citizens who live alone. And with so much violent crime in the news, security has really become a hot topic these days. Could we try it next Thursday the tenth, or would Wednesday the sixteenth be more convenient for you?"

Objection: "We use our own research staff to line up our guests."

Rebuttal: "I can certainly understand your wanting to use your own people, but we are offering a unique and very unusual personality with an interesting story to relate. Do you want to schedule an appearance for next week, or would later in the month be better?"

Objection: "Send a press kit."

Rebuttal: "I'll be glad to put a press kit in the mail for you today, and if you like I'll include a few sample questions your host may want to review for ideas of her own. Should I call back Thursday to answer questions, or would Friday morning be a better time for you to talk on the phone?"

Direct Recruiting Call

PO: "Jim, this is John Truitt. I'm working on an important executive search assignment involving a very lucrative opportunity that you ought to know about. Could we get together for a confidential interview in my office this afternoon, or would tomorrow morning be more convenient for you?"

Question: "How much does it pay?"

Rebuttal: "The company will pay whatever it takes to hire the ideal candidate. Would you like to meet me for a quick cup of coffee this afternoon, or can you wait until tomorrow morning to learn all the details?"

Objection: "I'm happy where I am now."

Rebuttal: "Well, I'm sure you are, but wouldn't you be a lot happier with an even better job that allowed you to bring home more money for your family, too?"

Objection: "I'm expecting a raise in six months."

Rebuttal: "That's great, but if we get together soon I can show you how you may have an even better raise immediately, and start taking home those larger paychecks six months sooner. Would you like to stop by my office on the way home from work this evening, or is tomorrow afternoon more convenient for you?"

A First Date

PO: "June, this is Bill Thomas. I think it's time we got to know each other better, and wondered if you'd like to meet me at Todd's for dinner tomorrow evening around seven o'clock. Or would Wednesday night be better for you?"

Objection: "I'm sorry, Bill, but I don't go out with people I don't know that well."

Rebuttal: "That's why I thought we should meet in a public place like Todd's, first. We'll see what we have in common and enjoy a great dinner at the same time. Do you want to try it tomorrow night, or would later in the week be better for you?"

Objection: "I don't know if I should."

Rebuttal: "I know exactly how you feel because I don't like blind dates either. Why not bring a friend along with you? If we have a good time, we can do it again. If not, it won't be because we didn't give it a chance. Which is better for you—tomorrow night or later in the week?"

Arranging an Appointment for a Sales Presentation

PO: "Jack, this is John Truitt with Telestar Inc. I'd like to meet with you in your office to discuss some ways we can help your employees increase sales and profits with better phone skills. Would tomorrow afternoon be a good time for you, or would later in the week be more convenient?"

Objection: "Business is too slow now for us to consider any new purchases."

Rebuttal: "I know slow times can be killers, but maybe we can come up with some new ideas for speeding up business with more sales. Could we get together tomorrow, or would Thursday be better for you?"

Objection: "I don't think we'd be interested."

Rebuttal: **"I'm sorry for not explaining it better, but if we can get together I will show you some very interesting ways to increase your sales and profits. Could we meet in your office tomorrow afternoon to discuss this further, or does early Thursday morning look better on your schedule?"**

Objection: "I'm too busy."

Rebuttal: **"I can certainly understand the restraints of a tight schedule. In fact, saving time to improve productivity is one of the greatest benefits of our programs. Do you mind waiting until next week to learn more about this, or would you rather try and find a way to get together sooner?"**

Arranging Employment Interviews

PO: **"Hank, my name is Mary Wilson. I'm a software design engineer with seven years of experience at a major communications firm here in Houston, and would like to arrange an interview in your office to discuss working for you. Would tomorrow afternoon be convenient, or would next Monday morning be better for your schedule?"**

Objection: "We're not hiring now."

Rebuttal: **"Yes, I heard you had a fine organization. In fact, that's the main reason I wanted to meet with you. Could we try it later this week, or would the first part of next week be more convenient for you?"**

Objection: "Send a résumé."

Rebuttal: **"I'd be glad to, Hank, but I haven't even had a chance to put one together for you. Could I bring it with me to an interview tomorrow afternoon, or would Friday be better for you?"**

Setting up an Audition

PO: "Joe, this Mary Taylor. My act has been packing the house for a comedy club in Dallas, and I'd like to set up an audition for an opportunity to perform in your club. Will you be free tomorrow afternoon, or is Thursday better for you?"

Objection: "We can't afford expensive talent."

Rebuttal: "I can't blame you for watching expenses, but an experienced performer can help increase your profits by attracting more customers, and then bringing them back again and again. Is Thursday afternoon too early for an audition, or would Friday be better for your schedule?"

Objection: "We find our own acts."

Rebuttal: "I realize you are known for attracting good talent, and if you are the one who discovers me in Houston, your reputation should be enhanced even more. Can we try an audition tomorrow, or would you rather set it up for Monday instead?"

Arranging Appointments with Loan Officers or Investors

PO: "George, this is Bill Thomas with the XYZ Company. I'd like to arrange an appointment to meet with you in your office to discuss a very profitable business opportunity for both of us. Would tomorrow afternoon be convenient, or would later in the week be better for your schedule?"

Objection: "Send a prospectus or business plan."

Rebuttal: "I'd be glad to, but since I'm a better businessman than I am a writer, I'd like to go over the details with you in person to answer any questions, and show you how we've already started turning a profit. Could we try it later on this week, or would Monday be a better day for you?"

Question: "What kind of investment did you have in mind?"

Rebuttal: "That will depend upon several factors we'll need to talk about in confidence. Could we meet tomorrow, or would you rather do it a little later in the week?"

Objection: "We don't normally do business with people we don't know."

Rebuttal: "That's why I thought we should meet as soon as possible, so you could get to know me, review our references and see how much progress we've already made. Which looks best on your calendar—Thursday morning or early Friday afternoon?"

Arranging Interviews with Newsmakers

PO: "John, my name is Mary Porter. I'm reporting on the most successful companies in our town for the <u>Business Chronicle</u>, and wondered if you would have time to give me a brief interview in your office tomorrow morning at 9:30. Or would right after lunch be better for you?"

Objection: "I don't like to give interviews because I'm always misquoted."

Rebuttal: "I know that kind of thing can be frustrating, but I'll promise to be as accurate as possible so our business readers understand your firm's success story. Can we try it tomorrow, or is Friday a better day for you?"

Objection: "Why should I waste my time?"

Rebuttal: "Considering the opportunities such exposure can mean, you might want to <u>invest</u> a little of your time to tell your firm's story the way you want it told. Would later this week be a good time to meet, or would early the following week be more convenient?"

Objection: "Call our public relations representatives."

Rebuttal: "I'd planned on calling them for background material, but many of our readers are interested in what motivated you to start your business, and how you were

able to get it going so successfully in the beginning. If you feel a face-to-face meeting would take too much time, we could do the interview by phone tomorrow afternoon, or would the evening be better for you?"

Invitation to an Event

PO: "Mr. White, this is Tesia Truitt from Askew Elementary School. We're having a band concert and dance show in our auditorium next Thursday night at eight o'clock to benefit homeless families in our community. The tickets are only $4.00 apiece, and all the proceeds go to feed the homeless. Can you and your family come watch me dance in the concert, and do you have more friends who might attend as well?"

Objection: "We contribute for those kinds of things at the office."

Rebuttal: "Oh, that would be great if you could bring your entire office. How many tickets would your company want to buy?"

Objection: "No, we really wouldn't be interested."

Rebuttal: "I'm sure you're busy with other things, Mr. White, but these families really could use all of our help. Could you just buy tickets for your family so they could come to the concert?"

Objection:"You are very persistent."

Rebuttal: "Yes, sir, I do believe in what we're doing, and it should be a great concert. Wouldn't you like to join other families in our neighborhood who are trying to help, too?"

Obviously when you are inviting a Priority Contact to a one-time-only event, you can't offer him a choice of two time slots. You then have to focus more on selling the benefits of attending the event itself.

A friendly, cheerful Telestyle will not only make all these Power

Openers and rebuttals sound more accommodating. It will also help soften any selling techniques you may have to use as well.

Turn Positive Questions into Appointments

If an employer starts asking a job hunter questions about his background, one can assume the employer has an opportunity in mind. Likewise, prospects who ask questions about a salesperson's products or services are showing "buying signals" of interest. The same may be said for other questions from a prospect. Whenever a talk-show producer wants to know more about a guest, an investor asks questions about a business opportunity, or a potential dinner date starts asking what the caller has in mind for the evening, these are all positive questions that show interest.

Whenever you receive such a positive inquiry, follow Truitt's Law to go ahead and answer the question, but finish your answer like this:

> **Caller: ". . . But I'm on a private line right now, and could answer all of your questions a lot more freely in your office than I can on the telephone. Could we meet tomorrow morning at ten o'clock, or would right after lunch be better for you?"**

If you stretch out the conversation to try to answer all the Priority Contact's questions, you may talk yourself out of the appointment.

If you must meet with your Priority Contact face to face, in order to accomplish all of your goals, don't say too much on the phone. Just get the appointment, add whatever details you need, and get off the line.

Arouse the Priority Contact's curiosity, and you have given him a strong incentive to meet with you. *Satisfy* that curiosity, and the Priority Contact may then feel there is no reason to meet with you personally. Listen for these "buying signals," but convert those positive questions into appointments quickly.

Handle Details Professionally

If you are in sales and need to qualify your prospect *after he or she has agreed to an appointment*, handle it this way:

> **Caller: "Before we get off the line, let me ask you a couple of quick questions to help prepare for our meeting and save more of your time, too. Can you tell me how many employees you have working in your office now, Jack?"**

Use the same method to obtain directions for locating the Priority Contact's office. If you are interrupted or feel you have already taken up too much of the Priority Contact's time on the phone before obtaining directions, call his secretary back later . . .

> **"Hi, Judy, this is John Truitt. I have an appointment with Jack tomorrow, and wondered if you could give me directions for driving to your office from downtown?"**

Note the appointment in your date book, on your Priority Call Planner, or Telesearch List if you are using one, along with any other pertinent information or facts you learned during the call. Then pick up the phone and call the next person on your list.

Remember to Get Something from Every Call

Follow the guidelines for planning and carrying out a successful Telesearch, and use your best phone skills with each and every call. Keep the Call Review Checklist (Figure 2) beside you when placing your calls, to remind you of all the skills and tactics at your disposal. Prepare rebuttals for the ten worst or most difficult questions and objections you might hear, and practice saying them with feeling until you are ready for anything.

Don't forget that the Priority Contact's first question or objection may simply be a meaningless ploy to hold you off for a second while he collects his thoughts. Handle that all-important first question or objection smoothly, as shown in the previous examples, and refocus the conversation upon the most convenient time to meet. Use at least three rebuttals with each Priority Contact, but if you are unable to arrange an appointment . . .

Switch to the indirect approach to ask for referrals.

The indirect approach goes something like this:

Caller: "Well, Jack, I do appreciate your taking the time to chat with me on the phone, and I am sorry we won't get a chance to meet. I wonder if you could at least help point me in the right direction. Who do you know who . . . ?"

Those who cannot meet with you may still be good sources of referrals in the future. If you have maintained a friendly, cheerful attitude throughout each conversation, many of your Priority Contacts will enjoy talking with you.

It will take less than a minute for Priority Contacts to realize they don't know you, but by then (if you handle yourself properly) they will like you anyway.

People are more than helpful to people they like. You will not only get all the appointments you need, but you should also have a good time making new friends and worthwhile business contacts for the future, too.

Who Will Win?

Along about now, if not sooner, I usually get a question in my seminars and public appearances like, "All this sounds great, John, but what happens when we run into secretaries, screeners, and Priority Contacts who have also read your book and know the same rebuttals and Teletactics we know?"

The stock answer is that those should be the friendliest, most enthusiastic, and inquisitive telephone conversations on record—*if and when both parties have practiced and mastered their skills and techniques to perfection.* Reality teaches, however, that one reader will have worked harder, practiced longer, and will be more alert and persistent than the other.

Most calls to Priority Contacts take no longer than three to five minutes each, and most conversations with screeners last no more than fifteen seconds. Thus, whoever is more alert, better prepared and puts forth the best effort will always win.

That's what INSTANT INFLUENCE is all about—controlling the instant, those brief seconds or minutes it takes to complete each call. Whoever masters these skills and techniques is going to sound friendly, intelligent, confident, alert and very professional on the telephone.

Professionalism always earns respect.

Skills and techniques can't do everything, of course. At some point your objectives will have to stand up under close scrutiny and evaluation on their own merits. But phone skills can help you reach the people you want to, and communicate your message to whoever you believe should hear it so you have every chance of influencing those people. After that you're on your own.

If you believe in what you're doing, put in the time and effort to practice the skills, strategies, tactics, and techniques you will need for success.

The dialogues, Power Openers, and rebuttals you learn from the examples in this book will not sound "canned" or memorized if you are honest and speak from the heart with enthusiasm. If the words you say and the enthusiasm you use to say them are genuine, it will not matter what kind of training the other party has had, because you can train yourself better, (if you care enough to put in the effort), and the "numbers" are in your favor.

Even the most effective techniques will never work all of the time, but if you make enough calls, they will work most of the time—more than enough to ensure your success in any endeavor.

8

THE POWER OF
INSTANT INFLUENCE

B y now you should realize that the telephone will help you save time and money doing virtually anything. This is particularly true for someone with the entrepreneur spirit, who wants to use the telephone to start and manage a successful business.

INSTANT INFLUENCE for Entrepreneurs

If you have the kind of hardheaded determination it takes to convert an idea into a successful business, the telephone can play a major role in that success. It can help you save time gathering information, obtaining legal advice, finding out about licensing, searching for the right location, obtaining discounts for equipment, supplies, and materials, prospecting and closing sales, improving customer relations, managing accounts receivable, recruiting key people, arranging promotions and publicity, and much, much more.

Those interested in purchasing all or part of an existing business can implement a Telesearch Plan for that purpose alone. Prepare a Telesearch List of the presidents or owners of any companies or existing businesses in your field of interest. Then use an indirect approach:

> **Caller: "Frank, my name is Jack Thompson. I'm seriously thinking of investing in a business like yours, and wondered if you might know anyone interested in selling, or taking on a new partner with capital to invest?"**

Any of my readers who have been entrepreneurs will attest to the fact that a Power Opener like this one will get the kind of attention you want. The indirect approach may also be used to learn about existing competition, to identify the concerns of those already in the kind of business you are investigating, and to gather valuable inside information that will help you evaluate the future outlook for success.

Almost any response from the Priority Contact to a Power Opener like the one shown above should be helpful. It is fairly easy to predict initial responses and prepare effective rebuttals to focus the conversation wherever you want it to go:

Obj: "I'm not interested in selling my business."

> **REB: "I'm sorry, Jack, I must not have made myself clear. I never suspected you might be interested in selling your business, but I was hoping you might know a competitor who needed help, wanted to get out, or could use a boost of new capital and energy to expand his operations. Does that sound like anyone you know?"**

Obj: "I can't think of a soul."

> **REB: "Well, I do appreciate your taking the time to talk with me. Can you think of anyone I might call who might be able to point me in the right direction?"**

Quest: "Why should I help a competitor?"

> **REB: "Well, you certainly don't have to, but I'm sure there's**

enough business out there for everyone. I just thought that as a leader in the industry you might have friends among the competition, and would know if any of them could use the kind of help I'm offering?"

Quest: "I might be interested; what kind of deal are you looking for?"

REB: "That will depend upon the size of the business and what's involved. Would you like to set up a time later on this week for me to tour your facilities, and then talk privately over lunch? Or would the early part of next week be better for you?"

Resp: "Why don't you call Andy Brown at Kingfish Enterprises? His partner, George Stevens, recently retired, and he might be interested in taking on a new one."

REB: "Andy Brown at Kingfish Enterprises. Thanks for the lead. Can you think of anyone else I might call?"

Get as many names as you can first, then obtain contact information and ask whatever questions you want as to business history, reasons for selling, etc.

Before investing your life savings and eighteen hours per day in starting a new business, why not research the markets by calling potential customers, too? Who normally purchases the products or uses the services you want to offer? Once prepared, such a Telesearch List will not only be useful for market research, it can also be used for prospecting and selling later on, too. Use the Priority Call Planner (Figure 1) to plan your calls, list all the questions you wish to ask, and prepare for whatever questions or objections you may expect from Priority Contacts. Then use the same Power Opener one might use for comparative shopping by phone:

Caller: "Mary, my name is John Truitt. I'm conducting a little private research project, and wondered if you might be able to recommend a good graphics company for designing letterheads, brochures, logos, etc. Do you use an outside firm for this kind of artwork, and if so would you recommend them?"

You may prefer using the term "private research project" instead of "survey," because the word "survey" has been so abused by salespeople in recent years that it can cause undue suspicion. Many Priority Contacts will be more open if they believe you are working on a project for yourself instead of your employer or a competitor.

A "Private Research Project" could be for anything, and eliminates the need for mentioning the name of your business or organization.

Although the phrase "private research project" could honestly describe an assignment you are working on professionally, it could just as truly be something you are doing for yourself. It certainly has an unlimited variety of applications. When you find a cooperative Priority Contact, seize the opportunity to learn what your future customers value most when doing business with the kind of firm you hope to start.

> **Caller: "How much do they normally charge for their services? . . . .**
>
> **Do they offer any services that are unique? . . .**
>
> **Do you know what kind of equipment they use? . . .**
>
> **What impresses you most about them?"**

Just ten or more conversations with potential customers like these, who purchase the kinds of products or services you intend to offer, can help you learn what appeals to them, the kinds of rates or prices paid, and what customers want. Such information can be invaluable for estimating your chances of success, planning advertising and sales literature, pricing, etc. Of course any Priority Contacts who say they are disappointed with your future competitors' services or products, or that they cannot recommend a certain firm, should be earmarked for sales calls once your business gets started. They will be prime prospects for those crucial first sales you will need to get your fledgling enterprise off the ground.

These tactics can be just as valuable for existing businesses that are considering expanding into new markets, helping to locate a variety of low-price vendors and suppliers of artwork, printing, office furniture, equipment, materials, supplies, space, etc.

Every dollar saved on start-up expenses will help you stay in business that much longer during those typically lean start-up months.

We'll discuss more comparative shopping methods later in this chapter, but can you see how the instant availability of virtually any information you want can be invaluable in helping you make the right decisions? Now let us explore more ways of influencing other people's decisions, too.

Put Telesearch into Your Sales Strategy

We have already discussed techniques for handling telephone orders and inquiries, selling add-ons, asking for referrals, qualifying prospects, closing sales, prospecting by Telesearch, and arranging appointments for sales presentations. The Telephone Sales Test described in Chapter 4 can be used to select products and services to be sold through outbound phone calls as well as with incoming calls, too.

Some firms give each salesperson a little three-sided cubicle with a desk, telephone headset, and computer terminal or file cabinet. Others prefer the "open concept," with two to four desks grouped together in "islands" in a large room. The cubicles offer a little more privacy and shield against background noises, but the open concept is less confining. A private office, of course, is best of all, but one may economize and still retain a certain degree of privacy by allowing two salespeople to share the same office. Those seriously considering a large operation should also investigate the newer telemarketing computer software package and telecommunications systems.

Smaller firms may simply ask their outside sales reps to spend a few hours each week on the phones, while others can use an "inside sales desk" for training new salespeople, by letting them work the phones initially in order to familiarize themselves with customers, products, and services before making outside sales calls. Some of the smallest firms let secretaries earn extra income in commissions during slow times by prospecting and arranging appointments for their sales reps, or actually selling certain products and services by telephone themselves. I've also helped a number of retail operations set up a system of having their salespeople call prior customers and other prospects during periods of slow floor traffic to invite them into the stores for specials, etc.

> **Caller: "Bill, this is Mark Matteau at Mr. Carpet. We're having a gigantic sale on our entire inventory of luxury carpeting this weekend, and I wanted to invite you and Alice to come in Saturday morning. Or would Sunday afternoon be better for you?"**

Those who are not interested themselves can be excellent sources of referrals:

> **"Well, I did want to give you the first crack at this deal because we consider you one of our most valued customers, but if you're not interested, perhaps you can recommend someone else. Who do you know who would appreciate saving up to 40 percent on the finest brand-name carpeting and having it installed free of charge, too?"**

If you are enthusiastic describing your offer in an indirect approach when asking for referrals, the prospect you are talking to may change his mind.

> Prospect: "Well, Mark, on second thought maybe Alice and I could come in Saturday morning. That does sound like a good deal, and we still have a couple of guest rooms to carpet. Will you be there around eleven?"

If you want to sell products or services by phone that pass the Telephone Sales Test, you will need a prepared script that includes a Power Opener, commitment questions, rebuttals, and a closing strategy. But, remember, *the entire conversation should last no more than five minutes.*

You and your sales force will be much more successful on the telephone if you call *first*, before mailing product literature or brochures, instead of sending out mass mailings to be followed up with phone calls.

Many prospects will want you to send information before they agree to buy, but if you wait until such data is requested, you will not only save money on direct mail expenses, but your material will receive more of the attention it deserves. Many secretaries and consumers throw away unsolicited mail with hardly a glance. However, if your brochure or product literature is requested, you may then begin the accompanying cover letter with a phrase like, "Enclosed please find the information you requested during our telephone conversation this afternoon . . ." Such a personalized letter and the material enclosed with it will normally be passed on to your Priority Contact without delay.

If you call first, you will avoid any distraction caused by referring to previous correspondence. Depending upon the type of product or service you are selling you may actually close the sale without any preliminary correspondence at all. This is particularly true if you are selling a well known or brand name product which is instantly recognized.

Another typical telephone sales script might go as follows:

Sales: **"Kathy, this is Tommy Davis at Mt. Pleasant Travel. We've got a few tickets left for our young professionals' Hawaiian trip planned for the week of March fifth through the thirteenth, and I wondered if you knew any couples or single people who might be interested in a substantial discount on a complete package including meals, lodging, and round-trip air fare?"**

Prospect: "I might be interested, since I'll be on spring break that week. How much are the tickets?"

Sales: **"Normally a vacation like this would run $2,000, but if** you go with our group, the discount reduces the total cost to only $1195. We'll all be staying at the Surfrider right on the beach, and there are plenty of island tours, parties, shopping sprees, and other activities planned for couples and single people alike. Would you like for us to bill you for your ticket, or would you prefer to charge it on your VISA or Master Card?"

Prospect: "Gosh, Tommy, I'm not sure. Can you send me a brochure?"

Sales: "I'd be glad to, Kathy, but I've only got a few tickets left, and we need to complete all reservations as soon as possible to get the discount. Why not let me reserve a ticket with your credit card, and I'll put a brochure in the mail to you today. You will have two weeks to cancel if you can't go, but if you can, you'll save $800 on a fabulous week in Hawaii. Does that sound good to you?"

Prospect: "I think I'd better look at your brochure first before making any kind of commitment."

Sales: "I don't blame you for being cautious, but I'm sure you'll love this trip, and I hate to see you miss an opportunity to save $800 on a Hawaiian vacation. Can you imagine how much fun you can have in the islands with an extra $800 in spending money for shopping?"

Prospect: "OK, I'm sold. Let me get my VISA card."

If you cannot close the sale without sending product literature first, go ahead and mail or fax the information requested to your prospect, but include a statement like the following in the accompanying cover letter:

"Please review these brochures at your leisure and expect to get a call from me later on this week."

This is much better than requesting the prospect to call you after reviewing your printed material, because it leaves the initiative to you. Thus you stay in control and can plan your time accordingly. Mentioning a precise time when you will call back may help motivate the prospect to review your material immediately, so he or she will be ready for your call.

Fax machines make it easy to get printed material to your prospects quickly, but if you have invested in expensive color brochures to help sell your wares, a few words of caution. Most fax machines will reduce your beautifully crafted literature to a black and white photocopy of questionable quality. Such a poor facsimile may destroy the impression you are trying to make and cost you a sale.

Run a test copy of any sales material you may want to fax to see how it will look to prospects. If it doesn't look good, either mail the original brochure or redesign your literature in black and white for faxing.

Whether you mail or fax information to a prospect, plan a follow-up call as soon as he has had a chance to review it. In follow-up calls, instead of asking prospects if they have seen your literature (they will tell you if they have not), use an assumptive close. A Power Opener using an assumptive close should focus upon the best way to process the order.

"Hi, Jim, this is John Truitt at Telestar Inc. I wanted to follow up on the seminar information you requested after our last telephone conversation to see if we could plan a half-day program for your sales department next week. Or would the week after next be more convenient for your group?"

Some sales professionals prefer the Negative Statement Multi-Point Close when selling more expensive products or services.

(Negative Statement)

Caller: "Kathy, if I really thought this trip was not the kind of thing you'd like, I wouldn't suggest it for you. I want you to come home afterward and tell all your friends what a great time you had, and send us some referrals, too. So before you make up your mind, there are a couple of questions you might wish to consider."

(Multi-Point Close)

"First, do you really believe you would enjoy a trip to Hawaii with other single professionals like yourself? Well if we got you an $800 discount, do you believe we'd be doing enough for you? And third, can you see how our easy pay plan makes it possible for anyone who really wants a great vacation like this to work it into his or her budget? Well, then, can you think of any logical reason why you wouldn't want to go to Hawaii with us this spring?"

Of course a vacation in Hawaii is not a difficult sale. Still the negative statement "I wouldn't even want you to consider," combined with multiple closing questions, can be used to help prospects make the buying decision on the spot.

Anyone with experience selling your products or services can tell you what questions or objections to expect from prospects. If you anticipate those points in advance, you will be able to prepare a Power Opener, commitment questions, and rebuttals that are effective. Review the rebuttals for sales situations in the previous chapters to help you come up with answers for virtually any objections you are likely to hear, and practice saying them over and over again until they sound natural coming from you.

The same closing techniques mentioned above can also be used in follow-up phone calls to those prospects who were presented face to face, but could not or would not make a decision when you were there. No prospect's desire for your product or service will ever be any stronger than when you first presented it, but you can still save some of those deals with follow-up calls.

Sales: "Jim, this is Marshall Conner with XYZ Systems. I wanted to follow up on our meeting last Thursday to see if we should go ahead and plan on installing your new inventory control system next month. Or did you want us to get started sooner?"

Prosp: "We like your proposal, Marshall, but I thought I'd see what your competition had to offer, too."

Sales: "I believe in comparative shopping myself but another

company's representative may not understand your needs like I do. The fact is, we have the best system money can buy in the price range discussed, and if you install our system, you know I'll be right on top of things to make sure everything is taken care of the way you want. Doesn't that sound better than having a bunch of strangers poking around in your business?"

Those prospects you cannot sell with a follow-up call may still be sources of referrals. A friendly, enthusiastic Telestyle combined with Power Openers that get to the point immediately can put you in the position to use all the selling and closing techniques you know. Just remember to listen for buying signals, control conversations with questions, and use Teletactics like the reverse and Truitt's Law to obtain the positive responses you want from prospects on the telephone.

If you manage a sales organization, have your salespeople role-play their techniques and dialogues among themselves until they are ready for anything. Working as a team, your group should be able to prepare Power Openers, commitment questions, and rebuttals that are "right on" because they know what to expect. As the leader you want to be sure each member of your team makes enough calls to line up the minimum number of presentations they will need to guarantee the net sales results you want. Most sales organizers figure it takes an average of three presentations to guarantee one sale, although the more experienced professionals' closing percentages will be considerably higher. It should be easy to review your organizations' weekly or monthly sales reports to come up with an accurate closing percentage for each member of your staff. Once you initiate a system that helps your people get all the presentations they need for success, then concentrate upon raising their closing percentages to increase their sales even more.

Follow-Up Calls Influence Better Customer Relations

Whether you are running a business from your home or are employed in sales for a multibillion dollar conglomerate, your ultimate success will depend to a great extent upon the kind of customer relations you are able to develop. Many sales professionals follow up each sale with a thank-you card or letter, and I would not say anything here to discourage the practice. I would however suggest . . .

A follow-up phone call after each sale can be more productive than a letter, because it allows misunderstandings to be resolved immediately, permits two-way communications, and provides an excellent opportunity to ask satisfied customers for referrals while they are still enjoying their purchases.

A thank-you call gives the salesperson a unique opportunity for the final "kiss," and further impresses his or her customer with a personal touch. Although your primary objective may be referrals, following up the sale with a thank-you call will make it appear to the customer that you are still interested in his or her satisfaction after the sale. Not only is this a great way to get referrals, but such calls also lay the groundwork for better customer relations in the future—and more repeat business.

If you continue servicing the same accounts, make notes about birthdays, names of children or associates, and other personal interests your customers have, so you will have reasons to stay in touch in the future. You may be surprised to find how many additional orders you can write on the phone by simply remembering to make such courtesy calls. Follow-up calls will also give you the opportunity to correct any misunderstandings or problems before they fester in the customer's mind and become insurmountable as time passes. Just as performers need to stay in touch with their audience, and politicians must remain close to their constituencies . . .

Businesses need to stay in close contact with their customers, so they may quickly adapt to changes in their needs.

Regular follow-up calls to your customers will also help you protect your valued accounts from the competition. It is very difficult to steal a satisfied customer from a sales pro who regularly takes the time to provide such personal attention to his clients' needs.

Phone Tactics for Managing Accounts Receivable

If you are extending credit to another business or consumer, you will of course want to check credit references. If your business belongs to the local credit bureau, one phone call to them should be sufficient. If you are not a member of a credit bureau or reporting service, you will need to check those references yourself. Be sure your credit application has a statement granting you permission to check credit references, and you should also verify that your customer has signed it. If there is any question about your rights and/or your customer's, consult your lawyer.

Credit laws are much stricter when it comes to protecting the privacy of consumers than that of businesses. So, I'll confine my remarks to business credit.

I should think the following questions about a business's credit standing would be permissable anywhere:

> **Caller: "Yes, Accounts Receivable? Who am I speaking with, please? Judy this is David Hinson at the XYZ Company. A firm named Gary Johnson & Associates has listed your company as a credit reference. How long has their account been open? The largest balance? Current balance? Can you tell me if they have a history of prompt payment of their invoices with your firm? Is their account current now? Have you ever had any trouble, or have they ever been more than thirty days delinquent?"**

Those who are familiar with credit laws may tell you only whether the customer's account is current or not. Some will tell you if they classify the account as "slow pay" or not. You will probably get a better idea of a customer's reputation if you talk with the owner of a small firm doing business with the customer than if you talk with a credit manager. Some entrepreneurs, less familiar with the law, may tell you more than they probably should.

> **Caller: "Bill, this is Paul Woodward at Kangaroo Exports. Bob Carter gave me your name as a business reference, and I wanted to ask you how he has handled his account**

> with you in the past. Would you consider him a good
> credit risk?"

Since the laws of the fifty states vary considerably concerning
credit reporting, not to mention federal laws . . .

**Check with your attorney to be sure your forms, questions,
practices, and the suggestions offered in this text are legal in
your area.**

I do know for sure . . .

**Any information you learn about someone's credit history
from a third party should be kept strictly confidential.**

One of the easiest ways to avoid collection problems with new
business accounts is with a regular contact schedule. Beginning
before you mail the first invoice, call the customer to verify all
details, prices, etc., before asking . . .

**Caller: "To whose attention should this invoice be addressed
so it can be taken care of immediately upon receipt?"**

Five days after mailing your first invoice to a new account, call
the customer's Accounts Payable Department, instead of the customer himself, to confirm receipt of your invoice and inquire when
it is scheduled for payment. Make a note of the name of the person
you talk with and his or her extension for future references. Then
wait no longer than five days after the date payment was promised
to place another *friendly* call to the person you previously spoke
with in Accounts Payables to "check on the status of the invoice."
I prefer handling collection matters with a firm's Accounts
Payable Department rather than the customer himself, in order to
avoid irritating someone who may well be, and continue to be, a
valued client in the future. Normally Accounts Payable will know
more about it anyway. The only time you may want to call the
customer instead of Accounts Payable is if the invoice has not been
approved or released for payment, or when the account becomes
seriously delinquent.

If companies know you are on top of your receivables and you are friendly during your inquiries, most will try to work with you to ensure prompt payment. If you have still not received payment within five days from the last date promised, it is time to take more assertive steps. But still use a friendly Telestyle.

> **Caller: "Mary, this is Don Dodsworth with National Health Foods. I was surprised to learn that we still haven't received your check for the invoice we discussed last month. Have you already sent that out, or should I drop by your office this afternoon to pick it up myself?"**

If the other party says "the check's in the mail," or "the computer is down," give him or her the benefit of the doubt and wait another five days before calling again. If you get the same story the next time you call . . .

> **"Oh, that's great. Can you give me the check number and date it was mailed so I can get my accountant off my back, please?"**

If you are given a number, let it rest. If the other party cannot give you a check number, offer to help out yourself in a friendly manner without accusing the other party of lying to you.

> **"I know how hectic things can be, but my accountant is giving me a hard time, and I have to pay attention to what she says. I think I can help if you will just stop payment on the check you mailed, and I'll run by your office later on this morning and pick up a new check myself. Or would right after lunch be better for you?"**

If this doesn't work, you have a collection problem on your hands. Then try calling the customer.

> **"Hi, Jim, this is Paul Woodward. You may not know it, but your accounts payable department has still not paid us for the merchandise you purchased six weeks ago. We understand how mistakes can be made, but it will avoid**

problems if you'll have a check ready for me to pick up by eleven o'clock this morning. Or would after lunch be better for you?"

If this doesn't work, call the president or owner of the firm (if not the customer himself) and explain, using a friendly Telestyle, that you are willing to come pick up his company's check yourself, rather than get lawyers involved in what is obviously an oversight. If this last attempt fails, have your lawyer write a letter for you on his or her letterhead.

Whatever you do, don't get into a heated discussion or make threats.

If you lose your temper, you lose.

Sure, an outburst may vent your frustrations, but it will also anger the debtor—sometimes so much that he or she will never pay until a court orders it, and that could take two years or more. If a debtor is having troubles and is honest with you, by all means work with him or her not only to collect the debt, but also to save a customer for future business once those financial difficulties have passed. If you are offered a partial payment, take it. But also ask for a firm promise as to when the balance will be paid and write it down. I know it sounds like a lot of hassles, but if you work closely with the slow account until it is up to date, you will be better off in the end.

Most problems may be avoided entirely if you take the time to check references before extending credit, and follow the contact schedule described in this text until you are familiar with each new account's payment procedures.

Managers Can Motivate with Telestyle

The Priority Call Planner (Figure 1) can be used to manage all kinds of projects and check up on employees' activities from your office by telephone. Fax machines, electronic mail, and other computerized telecommunications systems make it possible to have reports and other data on your desk instantly, so you may review them with employees on the phone as soon as they are received, or even as they are being transmitted.

Practicing good Telestyle with enthusiasm on the telephone is an excellent way to improve employee productivity through motivation.

If you must correct an employee for a mistake, you will find your criticism and suggestions will be received and acted upon with a better spirit of cooperation if you begin and end each discussion with a friendly, enthusiastic Telestyle.

Begin each discussion with a friendly greeting before getting down to the nitty gritty. If you must criticize, do it quickly in precise, easy-to-understand language, and end each point with a question to be sure the employee comprehends what you are saying. Perhaps he has a solution of his own. Perhaps he agrees with and will implement yours. One tactic that works in any telephone discussion is . . .

Whenever you need further explanation of a statement, question, or suggestion from the other party, simply remain silent.

That silence can be deafening. It creates a vacuum, which prompts the other party to fill it with a elaboration on his or her earlier statement. Words like "Oh?" or "Really?" also encourage the other party to say even more.

When you must use forceful language to make a point with an employee, in order to shock him into realizing the error of his ways, do so quickly. But do not hang up the phone on an angry note, or without a commitment from the employee to take positive, corrective action immediately. If you end the discussion in a bad temper, you will only destroy the employee's productivity for the next hour or so—not to mention your own. You may also alienate the employee, lose his respect, and actually drive him to rebellion or vindictive action—none of which is productive.

Say what you have to say, but then (returning to a friendlier Telestyle) review the corrective measures with questions, to be sure the employee will carry them out with a positive attitude. Get excited as you portray the positive benefits (in addition to keeping his job) of making the corrections agreed upon, and you will motivate the employee to take such actions because he wants to, not just because the boss told him to.

We all perform much better when we want to do something than when we have to do it.

Remember to raise the volume and speed of your voice slightly to sound enthusiastic. Your own enthusiasm is far more effective than any threats you might ever make, and will virtually ensure that employees carry out your instructions, with the kind of positive, enthusiastic attitude that results in greater productivity.

How to Obtain Discounts on Virtually Anything

> Salesman: "I'd sure like to help you get this car. Let's write up the deal the way you want it, then give me a deposit to show the manager you are serious, and I'll see if I can talk him into approving it."

Sound familiar? It should, because the "third party close" is one of the oldest techniques in sales. The purpose of course is to make it appear the salesman is on your side while the sales manager is the bad guy. The salesman invariably returns with a statement like "Well sir, we're mighty close, but my manager says we still need a few hundred dollars more from you before we can close the deal."

Why not use a similar third party negotiating ploy yourself? Once you negotiate a price, ask the salesman to have his manager signify his or her approval on the sales order, but instead of giving him a deposit, tell him you want to take a copy of the sales order—with all options, accessories, finance charges, tax, title, and license fees, etc., included—to your banker or credit union to see if you can get a cheaper loan or pay cash. Then go home and start calling all the other dealers in your area to find a better price. Remember to talk to the owner or manager instead of another salesperson like this:

Caller: "Jim, this is Ray Jackson. I'm ready to buy a brand new car today if I can get a good discount from you."

(Give model, color, and list of equipment and accessories you want.)

"Do you have a car equipped like this in stock?"

Of course this procedure could be used for any kind of big-ticket items like computers, cellular phones, motorcycles, furniture, heavy equipment, office machinery, appliances, etc. If the owner or manager says he does have the same item in stock, start negotiating, but be prepared with rebuttals for the most common questions or objections you are likely to hear:

Question: "Why should I give you a discount?"

REB: **"Well, you certainly don't have to, unless of course you'd like to close a quick sale today without having to pay a commission or involving any other third party in the sale. Should I call another dealer, or are you interested making this sale yourself?"**

Question: "How much are you willing to pay?"

REB: **"I'm interested in the best deal I can find. Give me the lowest price you can live with, and I'll tell you if I'm interested."**

Objection: "We can't quote you a price over the telephone, but if you come into our showroom, I'm sure we can work something out."

REB: **"That's the way I'd do it if I could, but I just don't have time to visit every dealership in the area. I'm very serious and ready to buy a car today from whoever is most competitive. If yours is the lowest price, I'll be in your office this afternoon to close the deal. What's the best discount price you can offer to close a sale today?"**

You do not have to begin in a showroom if you already know the make, model number, and options you want, but you will probably need to see the item first before deciding upon the one you want. If you can learn everything you need to know from a few phone calls or a catalog listing, begin Telesearching for the lowest price, and then negotiate your best deal as shown above. One rule to remember is . . .

Get the other party to name his lowest price first, before you name a figure yourself.

Whoever names a price first usually loses, because the other party will believe that is the price to be negotiated. Once you are given a price, confirm that it includes everything you want in the way of options, accessories, warranties, etc., and then ask, "Does this price include sales tax and all other costs, or is there an extra charge for anything else?" If not, make sure the other party knows you want a "turn key" or "drive away" price that includes everything. Once you have that dealer's best price, call other dealers until you find the most competitive bid. Then call them all back to see if any will beat the lowest price you found, until you are satisfied that you've gotten the best deal of all.

This procedure may involve a couple of hours on the telephone, but if it saves you several hundred or even several thousand dollars, it should be worth the time invested. You can use the same procedure to save money buying virtually anything, whether you are purchasing for your home, church, a government agency, a charity, or your business. In addition to money, you will save time and hassles by negotiating on the telephone instead of fighting traffic by visiting all the dealers in town.

Solve Problems Quickly by Phone

If you have purchased a faulty product or are not receiving the kind of service you paid for, call the person in charge and use INSTANT INFLUENCE to solve the problem.

> **Caller: "The VCR you sold me does not work properly, and I'd like to have it replaced as soon as possible. Do I have to pay to bring it in myself, or can you send someone out with a replacement today?"**

Cooperate with the firm's customer-service people by answering whatever questions they may ask, but if you are not satisfied with the remedy offered . . .

> **"I'm sorry, but that is not satisfactory at all. May I speak with your manager, please?"**

Explain the problem again, and if you are still not satisfied, pursue it to the very top of whatever organization you are dealing with.

> **"I know you are trying to help, but that's just not good enough. Let me speak to your boss or whoever cares enough about your firm's reputation to correct this problem the way it should be. Is he in?"**

"Whoever cares enough about your firm's reputation" is the key phrase here, and may eventually lead you to the owner or president.

The higher up the chain of command you go, the more likely you are to reach someone with the power to make the right decisions or change policies to accommodate you.

If necessary, do not hesitate to talk to the chairman of the board of any company or business that has taken your money and given you a shoddy or faulty product in return, because (with few exceptions) the person at the top will care enough about his or her firm's reputation to make it right.

If problems with a company's customers cannot or will not be taken care of by lower level employees, it then becomes the responsibility of the person at the top.

Feel free to indicate that you are upset and disappointed with the quality of service you are receiving, but if you lose your temper, shout, use profanity, or make threats over the telephone you will get no help at all.

Keep your cool and maintain a friendly Telestyle, and you will receive cooperation from most of the people you talk with on the other end of the line.

If not, call your lawyer.

Reasonable discussions with the right decision makers are by far faster and cheaper than legal action.

The same techniques may also be used with local government agencies, too. If you cannot get the kind of help you need from employees or appointees, call the elected official in charge of the department or agency you are dealing with. Use a friendly Telestyle to suggest why the official you are talking to would prefer to have supportive voters rather than the local TV station's news team in your neighborhood.

> **Caller: "I realize this is not the kind of problem someone in your position should have to deal with, but a quick phone call from you should solve this problem without a lot of negative publicity, and should keep the voters in your district happier, too."**

Nothing works all the time, but the procedures outlined here should help with most companies and government officials—if you are in the right, and if you are dealing with people who are as honest as you are. If you cannot get the assistance you need by calling the decision makers yourself . . .

Reach out and Win Support for Your Cause

Sometimes it takes a little extra pressure to move giant corporations and government bureaucracies to take action. You can always organize demonstrations outside their offices, go door to door, or hang around shopping centers asking people to sign petitions, but such tactics are not only time-consuming, they are often ineffective.

Why not mobilize your forces faster by organizing a telephone campaign for INSTANT INFLUENCE instead? The following sample Power Opener and rebuttals should give you an idea of what I mean:

> **PO:** **"Hi, Sherry, this is Marisa. Most parents in the neigh-borhood are fed up with speeders who cut through our streets to avoid traffic during rush hours, so we're all going to call the Mayor's office and ask her to have stop signs erected before one of our children gets seriously hurt. Can we count on you to join us in calling tomorrow morning, or would you prefer to place your call in the afternoon?"**
>
> Quest: "What makes you think the mayor will listen?"
>
> **REB:** **"The mayor might not listen to only one or two complaints, but she has to pay attention to a hundred or more phone calls in one day. We've got seventy-eight volunteers lined up so far, and if you and Bill will each make a call, that will bring it to eighty. Can you see how this kind of effort could make a difference?"**
>
> Quest: "What if they won't put my call through?"
>
> **REB:** **"Just tell her secretary why you are calling. Or, even better, tell her you don't mind holding until the mayor is free to talk to you. Don't you think she'll get the point with a hundred angry voters tying up the telephone lines?"**
>
> Obj: "I don't know if we should get involved."
>
> **REB:** **"I can understand your hesitation, but a quick phone call doesn't require very much involvement, and could help make our neighborhood a safer place to live. Can you and Bill each make a call tomorrow morning, or would you rather do it in the afternoon?"**

If your cause is worthwhile, you will not have much trouble gathering support, because a phone call requires only three to five minutes involvement by each participant. Even the most apathetic of citizens can be persuaded to invest a couple of minutes of their time in a cause if they believe in it, and can see how their efforts could make a real difference.

These kinds of tactics can also be effective for arousing the interest of the media in an issue, for getting the largest of corporations to modify its policies to protect the environment or the safety of its employees, or for revising actions that affect the local community, etc.

A telephone campaign such as the one described can be initiated by one person calling all the people he or she knows, who in turn call their friends, who then enlist the support of the people they know, and so forth and so on, until a small army of supporters is mobilized in record time. Such a mass effort can tie up phone lines and get the attention of even the most cumbersome bureaucracies. Do you see how you or anyone else can use INSTANT INFLU-ENCE to make a difference?

The telephone has been used for years by political organizations and charities to garner support and raise money for a variety of causes, too.

> **Caller: "David, this is Sally Funke. We need a $100 contri-bution from you to help Ed Buckley get elected to Congress this fall. Or could you contribute more?"**

> **"Debbie, this is Marshall Currance with the Charleston Historical Society. We're trying to raise money to reno-vate the old fire station on Meeting Street, and I won-dered if we could depend on you for at least $25. Or could you make a larger donation for a worthwhile project like this?"**

Whatever your cause, the telephone is by far the fastest way to enlist support. Those who cannot provide financial support or participate themselves should be good sources of referrals. If you follow the Telesearch strategies, you can plan an effective cam-paign to increase support or achieve any worthwhile goal. Once again . . .

The best way to influence others to take action, contribute money, or participate in your cause is to use enthusiasm when talking with them on the telephone.

This bears repeating because the simple truth is as stated often before, *if you are excited, others will become excited, too*. You can keep that excitement going as long as necessary with enthusiastic follow-up calls on a regular basis to each volunteer, participant, or contributor until you have reached your goals.

Harness the Power of INSTANT INFLUENCE

Well, there you have it. All the skills, strategies, tactics, and techniques you need to use the telephone effectively in a variety of situations. If you follow the guidelines we have discussed, you should in fact know *whom to call*, *when to call*, *what to say* and *how to say it*—as well as the right Teletactics to use in any situation. Now it is up to you to pick up the phone and make this knowledge work for you.

Whatever task you set for yourself, it will be easy to influence other people because you will be communicating "brain to brain" on the telephone.

A friendly, cheerful, enthusiastic voice on one end of the line automatically stimulates a similar response from the party on the other end of the line, in a matter of seconds.

You can immediately harness this magic power to influence others if you remember to *control conversations with questions*, *maintain a positive mental attitude*, and *do not quit trying until you succeed*.

Reread Chapter 1 before you begin a new project, and take the time to plan and practice your Power Openers and rebuttals that seem appropriate, until you are fully prepared for whatever you might hear on the telephone—before placing your calls. If you have any problems, the Call Review Checklist (Figure 2) should help remind you of the skills you need to improve in order to solve those problems. Keep this book beside your phone for a quick reference, and review it as often as necessary to gain the skill and confidence you need for success.

If you are training others in these techniques, emphasize role-play sessions, so you and your trainees get plenty of practice among yourselves until everyone develops the skills they need for success. Be yourself on the telephone, but be the best self you can be. If you give it a 100 percent effort, you will not only avoid problems, but you should have a lot of fun making new friends and finding new ways to be more productive with the telephone by "smiling and dialing." Of course the real secret of INSTANT INFLUENCE is . . .

The more you use it, the more effective you will be.

DATE DUE

GAYLORD | | | PRINTED IN U.S.A.